Easy Programming
with C

Edward B. Toupin

Easy Programming with C

Copyright ©1994 by Que® Corporation.

Library of Congress Catalog Number: 94-67361

ISBN: 1-56529-888-8

96   95   94   4   3   2   1

Interpretation of the printing code: The rightmost double-digit number is the year of the book's printing; the rightmost single-digit number, the number of the book's printing. For example, a printing code of 94-1 shows that the first printing of the book occurred in 1994.

Screen reproductions in this book were created with Collage Complete from Inner Media, Inc., Hollis, NH.

Publisher: David P. Ewing

Associate Publisher: Joseph B. Wikert

Publishing Director: Steven M. Schafer

Managing Editor: Michael Cunningham

Product Marketing Manager: Greg Wiegand

Credits

Title Manager
Bryan Gambrel

Acquisitions Editor
Thomas F. Hayes

Acquisitions Coordinator
Patricia J. Brooks

Production Editor
Linda Seifert

Copy Editors
Wendy Ott
Maureen Schneeberger

Editorial Assistant
Michelle Williams

Technical Editor
Discovery Computing
Brian Stanek

Book Designer
Amy Peppler-Adams

Cover Designer
Jay Corpus

Production Team
Stephen Adams
Angela Bannan
Claudia Bell
Anne Dickerson
Karen Dodson
Chad Dressler
DiMonique Ford
Teresa Forrester
Beth Lewis
Nanci Sears Perry
Kaylene Riemen
Caroline Roop
Greg Simsic
Sue VandeWalle

Indexer
Michael Hughes

Composed in *Stone* and *MCPdigital* by Macmillan Computer Publishing

Dedication

To my grandfather Edward J. Pennison

About the Author

Edward B. Toupin is currently employed at a Denver-based engineering firm and has been a developer since 1983 in the finance, real estate, and oil and gas industries. He designs and develops applications under VAX/VMS, MS-DOS, and Microsoft Windows for real-time data acquisition, management, insurance claim management, and network management and communications. Ed is also the author of *Network Programming under VMS/DECNet Phases IV and V*. This is his first book for Que Corporation.

Trademark Acknowledgments

Contents at a Glance

Contents

Part 4: Variables and Constants — 56

Part 5: Functions and Macros — 68

Part 6: Mathematics — 82

Part 7: Comparing Data — 100

Part 8: Operations on Data · 116

Part 9: Decisions and Repetition · 140

Part 10: Screen Input/Output · 154

Part 11: File Input/Output 174

Index 194

Introduction

Have you ever wondered what goes on inside a computer program? Did you ever want to sit down at your keyboard and conjure up digital magic on your computer's screen? If so, there may be a computer programmer somewhere inside you, screaming to get out.

Unfortunately, you may have found computer programming not only intimidating but downright scary. If you feel this way, *Easy Programming with C* is here to give you basic knowledge about the C programming language.

Who This Book Is For

This book is for anyone who wants to learn to program their computer with C. More importantly, this book is for anyone who has flipped through other programming texts only to be discouraged by a foreign language and verbose explanation that leads the reader to drift off to never-never land. *Easy Programming with C* uses a conversational style in the explanations, along with short programming examples. Together, these elements take you right into the C language without any fear of getting lost in the jargon jungle.

Because its focus is on beginning programmers, *Easy Programming with C* is not a complete C reference—and therefore doesn't attempt to provide a comprehensive explanation of the techniques of professional programming. It merely provides you with a quick taste of C to pique your interest in programming. After reading this book, you will have a solid understanding of C programming fundamentals; you will be ready to move on to those more verbose texts and begin writing many useful and rewarding programs.

A Sample Lesson

This book is divided into 11 parts. Each part is then divided into several lessons. Each lesson is two pages in length and contains a short code segment and a brief line-by-line discussion of that code. Throughout this book, you will notice that a color scheme is used that makes each type of C word—similar to the parts of speech in a language—a different color.

Here is an example lesson:

Each lesson contains a short C-language code segment. You can run these programs on your C compiler as you work your way through the book.

Each code segment is broken down into numbered steps, which are then explained line-by-line.

Throughout this book, you will find small boxes of text, labelled "Note," "What Does It Mean?," and "Why Worry?" These boxes contain helpful information, definitions, and hints from the author that will help you through rough spots. New terms and emphasized words are presented in *italic* text; pay close attention to these terms.

LESSON 10

Integers

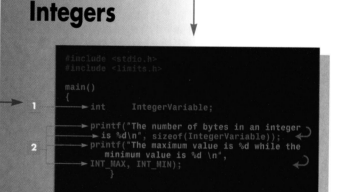

```
#include <stdio.h>
#include <limits.h>

main()
{
    int      IntegerVariable;

    printf("The number of bytes in an integer
        is %d\n", sizeof(IntegerVariable));
    printf("The maximum value is %d while the
        minimum value is %d \n",
        INT_MAX, INT_MIN);
}
```

The integer data type is used a lot in the C language for simple storage during the execution of a program. It is a numeric data type that provides for the storage of numbers. An unsigned int can range from 0 to 65,535 while a signed int, which is also the default for int, can range from –32,768 and +32,767.

WHY WORRY?

Occasionally you will have to break lines of code to fit onto a printed page, fit into your visible window, or fit within the boundaries of a compiler's established line width. These widths vary between 80, 132, and 256 characters across. The best place to break lines of code is at commas.

1 Declarations

For this program you only need one test variable of the int data type. The program declares the variable and the computer reserves 2 bytes of memory for IntegerVariable.

The int data type, as defined here, is a 2 byte data type that allows for the storage of numeric values ranging from –32,768 to +32,767. All variables declared to have the characteristics of the int data type are used in mathematical operations such as addition, subtraction, and multiplication.

WHAT DOES IT MEAN?

A *prototype* is a function definition that is used by the compiler to determine what parameters are required by the function as it is called in your program.

36

NOTE ▼

Due to space limitations in this book, we sometimes had to break code lines in illegal spots. To indicate two lines of code that must be typed on a single line, we have used a rev arrow (↵).

Lesson 10: Integers

Other definitions for int include signed and unsigned. An unsigned int stores values in the range of 0 to 65,535 and is available strictly for non-negative numbers. A signed int, also the default for the int variable defined here, has the same range as an int and is used for applications such as checkbook managers where negative numbers abound.

The int data type cannot support remainders, such as decimals generated in division operations. They are solely for the storage of whole numbers.

2 Output ◀

The output at this program section provides insight into the characteristics of the integer data type. The first printf() function prints the integer size using the sizeof() macro. The macro looks at the variable's data type and determines the number of bytes of that the data type uses.

The format string, text between the quotation marks, contains a text label and a format specifier. The text label provides output to the computer screen to identify the data. The %d is a *format specifier* that allows you to insert an int value into the output string. The \n is a carriage return line feed—similar to pressing the Enter key—placed in the output string to move the cursor to the next line after it prints to the screen. The value of the variable IntegerVariable is placed into the %d of the format string.

The second printf() statement prints the integer data type's minimum and maximum values. The definitions INT_MAX and INT_MIN are located in the limits.h include file and represent the maximum and minimum values allowed for an integer data type.

Like the previous printf(), the first %d prints the value of INT_MAX as an integer inserted into the format string while the second %d prints INT_MIN.

WHAT DOES IT MEAN?

A *macro* is a special type of routine and is called like a function. A macro provides a method of writing small segments of code that do not warrant writing a completely separate function.

A brief summary of each line of code, followed by a thorough explanation of what that line does, and how to use it in a program. Throughout the book, C terms appear in the same color scheme used in the program segments.

At the bottom of every lesson is a color-key that explains the colors used for the C terms. In each program listing and in the text of the lesson, preprocessor commands are purple, C reserved words are green, identifiers and symbols are red, strings and numbers are gray, and comments are yellow with a purple background. This same color scheme is used throughout the entire book.

Preprocessor   Reserved words   Identifiers and symbols   Strings and numbers   Comments   **37**

An Overview of the Book

Easy Programming with C is composed of eleven parts, each of which provides several lessons on different topics of the C language. Here is what you will find in each part:

- *Part 1* talks about the different C compilers on the market. You learn the advantages and disadvantages of each of the major compilers and see some sample screens of each.

- *Part 2* is a brief introduction to programming in the C language. In this part you learn, step by step, what is involved in writing a program in C.

- *Part 3* shows you the different data types of C. For each lesson you learn one of the different data types and how to work with it in a program.

- *Part 4* covers the uses of variables and constants giving you sample programs throughout.

- *Part 5* covers the important topics of functions and macros. You are given sample functions and macros to work with in each of the lessons in this part.

- *Part 6* covers mathematics in C. You do not have to be a mathematician to understand and use the concepts covered in this part.

- *Part 7* discusses the different methods of comparing data in C. Each lesson shows you the basics used in the decision making process of C.

- *Part 8* covers the many different operations on data in the C language. Moving, copying, and concatenating information are all covered in each lesson of this part.

- *Part 9* covers decisions and repetition. The lessons demonstrate how the C language makes decisions and executes commands based on those decisions.

- *Part 10* discusses screen-oriented input and output and how to communicate with your computer through the keyboard and monitor.

- *Part 11* covers file input and output as well as output to a printer. The lessons tell you how to read and write information to files on your hard drive as well as how to use a printer to print files.

Step Into the Wonderful World of C

Just around the corner is your first C programming lesson. We could stay here and chat all day, or you could turn the page and start on your fun-filled vacation in C-land. It is so easy you'll want to program all day—and drink coffee until three in the morning with brief breaks for ding-dongs and twinkies just like the rest of us! Have fun!

Turbo C++

Borland C++

Visual C++

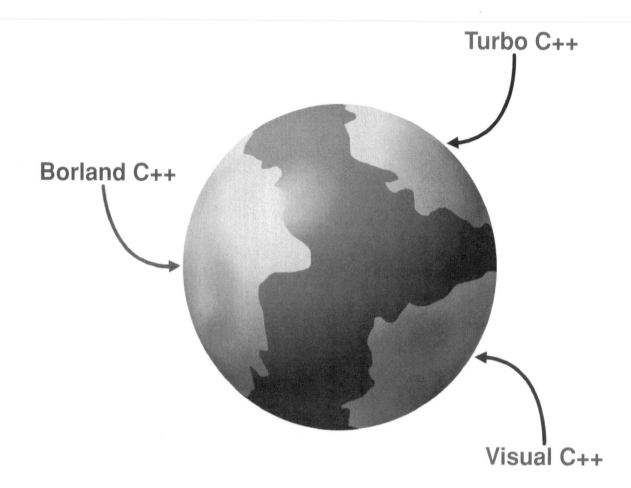

PART 1
Compilers of Choice

Before you can start programming in C, you have to get your hands on a compiler—but which one? There many vendors that produce compilers, but you have to decide for yourself which one you want to use.

Some of the compilers on the market are written for particular environments such as Microsoft Windows, DOS, Windows NT, UNIX, VMS, and other variations of operating systems and environments. The first thing you have to do is determine the environment you have and use that as part of your selection criteria. Do I have DOS? Windows? Which one do I use?

1 Borland C++

2 Visual C++

3 Turbo C++

Part 1: Compilers of Choice

The next step in your decision-making process is the level of C that you want to use. Again, with all of the vendors out there, each one might have an odd little variation of the ANSI C standards. This is not to say that all compilers do not follow ANSI C—they are all basically the same. It's just that some vendors add their own *special touch* to their compiler.

The next thing to look at is whether you want to be a professional programmer or just an everyday programmer. The flavors of C compilers out there come in two editions:

professional and standard. The standard edition enables you to write your programs and prepare them to run on your computer. Nothing fancy—just some nice, usable C programs.

The professional edition gives you programming libraries for everything under the sun as well as a great debugging application, a profiler, and sometimes a built-in wizard or an expert to take care of most of your code writing for you. The wizards and experts are discussed later in this lesson.

WHAT DOES IT MEAN?

ANSI stands for the American National Standards Institute. The institute establishes standards for many things in this country from eye protection to the C language standards.

WHAT DOES IT MEAN?

A *profiler* assists you in optimizing your program to make it more efficient.

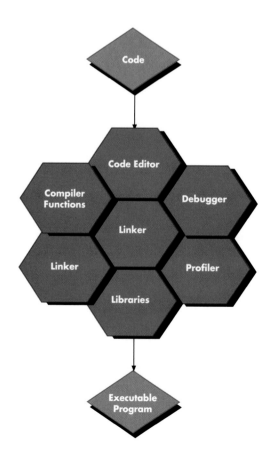

WHAT DOES IT MEAN?

A *debugger* helps you to step through your program and find errors that might cause your program to crash or cause erroneous results.

If you are absolutely sure that you want to program and are going to make it a living—choose a professional edition. If you are just going to learn C or are only going to be writing small utilities—go with the standard edition. The standard edition is much cheaper and easier to use.

One other thing to look at is, of course, the price. Compilers range from $90 to almost $1,000. Again, it all depends on what you want. Do you want to be a super-professional programmer or an everyday programmer? Do you want it all right now or can you settle for less and slowly add to your programming arsenal? If you want all of the programming libraries and utilities known to mankind and are ready to go with the programming biz—don't! Many of the utilities available you can do without for now—you can develop great applications with the less expensive compilers that give you a debugger and standard C. You will like yourself better in the morning.

These are not all of the choices involved in purchasing a compiler, but they are the more important ones. The rest of the decision is up to you. Are you a Microsoft, Borland, or Lattice fan? You have your own preferences to take into account as well.

Now read on and take a look at the more popular compilers on the market today. The first introduced is Borland C++ 4.0, the second is Microsoft Visual C++ v1.5 , and the final is Turbo C++. Read through the information on these compilers to assist you in your choice and good luck.

LESSON 1
Borland C++

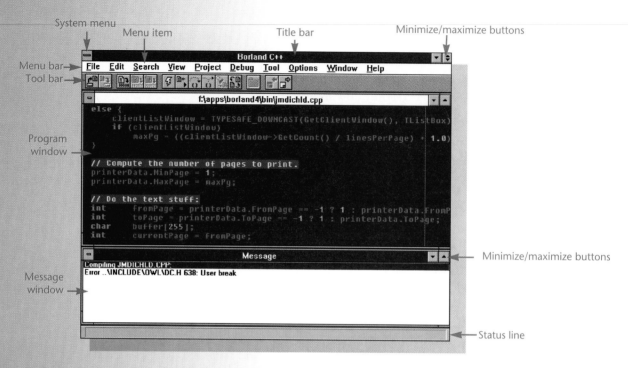

System menu · Menu item · Title bar · Minimize/maximize buttons
Menu bar · Tool bar · Program window · Message window · Minimize/maximize buttons · Status line

What Is It?

Borland C++ 4.0 (BC++) is Borland International, Inc.'s implementation of a C/C++ programming environment. It provides the capabilities of developing both standard C and C++ applications for 16/32 bit Microsoft Windows and DOS.

The Environment

The BC++ *integrated development environment*, IDE, is developed for the Microsoft Windows environment.

WHAT DOES IT MEAN?

An *integrated development environment*, IDE, is the environment in which you work in a compiler. The IDE contains menus, windows for program development, the C language compiler, and a linker.

The IDE has a standard Windows menu, but also supports a toolbar to easily access commonly used features of the system. The menu helps you to access all of the features of the environment such as managing projects, compiling, and accessing the compiler's tools.

WHAT DOES IT MEAN?

A *project* is an encapsulated set of files and libraries that make up an application. All of the files listed as part of a project contain code for your application. These files are compiled and linked together to create your final program to run on your computer.

The top window is the code window in which you enter your program into the environment. You can see that each portion of the program is color-coded to enable you to easily spot parts of the code. The bottom window is your message window. This window contains all messages, errors, and warnings that occur while your program is compiling and linking.

Features

The BC++ 4.0 environment comes with the IDE, as you see here, as well as a command-line version of the compiler. The IDE helps you to develop, compile, link, and debug your programs all in one simple environment. The command-line compiler helps you to compile your code outside of the IDE at the DOS command prompt.

Also included with BC++ 4.0 is the Borland Resource Workshop. This program helps you to develop Windows-based application dialogs, menus, bitmaps, and icons. These resources provide you with all of the essentials for developing a full-blown Windows application.

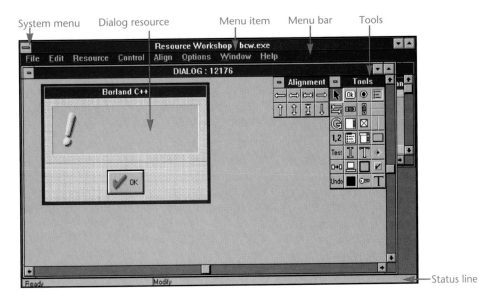

BC++ also contains what are known as *Experts*. Experts are used to help you develop your code. The *AppExpert* helps you chisel an application out of a predefined application frame. This frame is a set of codes that is generated by the expert, and all you have to do is fill in the blanks.

Also included is OWLObject Windows Library. This library provides an object-oriented approach to Microsoft Windows application development. All of the resources of a Windows application are encapsulated in a nice, neat little C++ object for ease of use.

As part of the environment, you also have a debugger that helps you go through your code and pick out any problem areas that can cause your application to crash. There is a Windows-based debugger and a DOS-based debugger to enable you to work in both environments.

Preprocessor   Reserved words   Identifiers and symbols   Strings and numbers   Comments

LESSON 2

Visual C++

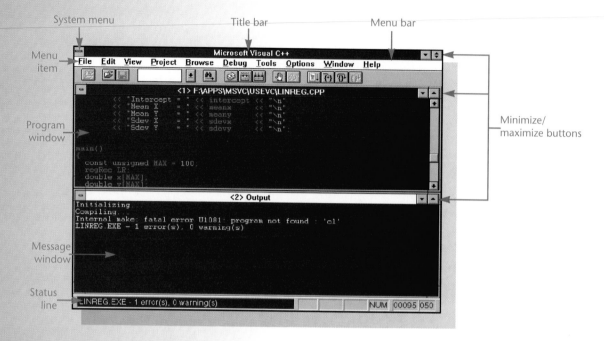

System menu · Title bar · Menu bar · Menu item · Program window · Message window · Status line · Minimize/maximize buttons

What Is It?

Visual C++ v1.5 is Microsoft Corporation's implementation of the C/C++ programming environment. As with Borland C++, it provides the capabilities of developing both standard C and object-oriented applications using C++ methodologies for 16/32 bit Microsoft Windows and DOS.

The Environment

The IDE has a standard Windows menu, but also supports a toolbar to access commonly used features of the system easily. The menu helps you access all of the features of the environment such as managing projects, compiling, and accessing the compiler's tools.

The top window is the code window where you enter your program into the environment. You can see that each portion of the program is color-coded and can be customized to whatever color scheme you desire.

The bottom window is your message window. This window contains all messages, information, errors, and warnings that occur while your program is compiling and linking.

Features

The environment comes with the IDE that you see here, as well as a command-line version of the compiler. The IDE helps you to develop, compile, link, and debug your programs all in one simple environment. The command-line compiler helps you compile your code outside of the IDE at the DOS command prompt.

Visual C++ contains *Wizards*. These Wizards help you develop your code. The AppWizard helps you build an application out of an application framework. This framework is code generated by the Wizard, providing you with the capability to go in and fill in the blanks to make a fully operational application.

Also included is Microsoft Foundation Classes (MFC). This library provides an object-oriented approach to Microsoft Windows application development in a manner similar to OWL.

The Resource Workshop mentioned for Borland C++ 4.0 is an integrated part of the AppWizard called *AppStudio*. This application helps you to create all of your dialog boxes and related Windows elements for Windows-based applications.

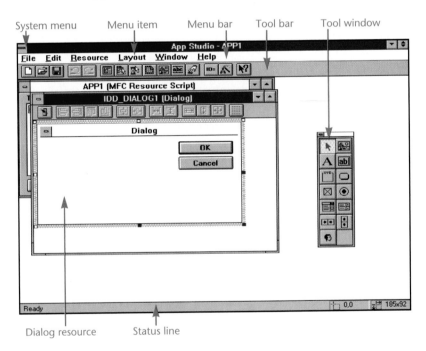

As with Borland C++ 4.0, you have a debugger that helps you go through your code and pick out any problem areas. There is a Windows-based debugger and a DOS-based debugger to enable you to work in both environments.

LESSON 3
Turbo C++

What Is It?

Turbo C++ is Borland International Inc.'s implementation of a standard edition C/C++ programming environment. It provides the capabilities of developing both standard C and object-oriented applications using C++ methodologies for DOS.

The Environment

The IDE is developed for the DOS environment. It has a menu, much like the Windows menus you have seen before, but it does not have a toolbar as in the Windows-based applications. The menu helps you access all of the features of the compiler easily. You can load and manage projects, compile and link, and execute the debugger from the one menu.

The top window is the code window where you enter your program into the environment. The bottom window is your message window that contains all errors and warnings that occur while your program is compiling and linking.

Features

The IDE helps you to develop, compile, link, and debug your programs all in one simple environment. The command-line compiler helps you to compile your code outside of the IDE at the DOS command prompt.

The standard version has no wizards or experts except for you. All code is generated by the user.

The environment does have a debugger for you to debug your code, but the utilities are provided to assist you in basic application development. Because the application runs under DOS, there is no need to have a workshop of any type to develop dialog boxes and menus. The DOS-based applications run under Windows in a DOS window, but not as part of the Windows operating environment.

The only libraries provided are those that enable you to create standard C/C++ applications. There are no additional libraries such as those provided with Borland C++ and Visual C++ application development.

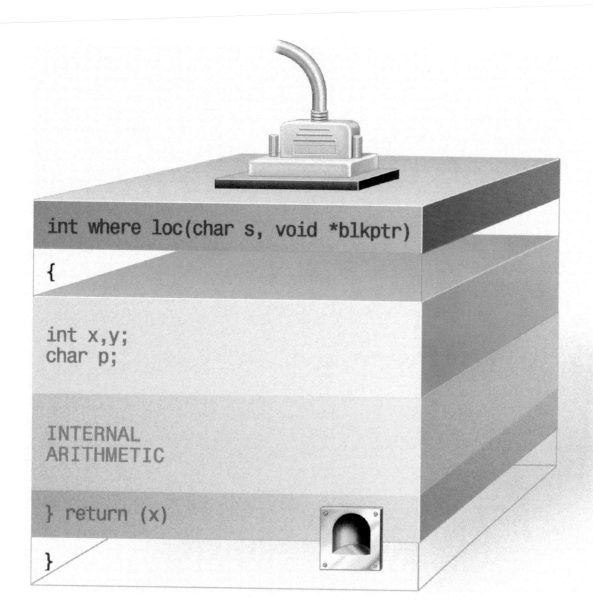

PART 2

Elements of a C Program

Before you delve into the topics in this book, it might help to have a basic understanding of what programming is all about. You already have a feel for what a program is and what it does, otherwise, your curiosity would not have been piqued enough to have bought this book.

There is one thing, though, that you should know before delving into the world of programming and the C language. No programmer would ever admit to it but—programming is easy! When you program, you are basically speaking a different language, like French or Spanish. Rather than talking to another human, you are using a machine, telling it what you want it to do for you.

One thing to remember while programming a computer is that it knows absolutely nothing until you tell it what it needs to know. It can do absolutely nothing on its own. Without a programmer to write some code to tell the computer what to do, the computer would simply sit there, burn electricity, and aggravate you because you spent all that money on a nice-looking box that hums.

When you program the computer, all you are doing is telling it how to perform a task that you already know how to do. So why bother? The reason is that it can perform endless calculations quickly without getting bored. After it is programmed, it can take over redundant tasks for you and you can carry on with your day without worry—until the electricity goes out!

Programmers are the people who tell computers what to do. That's not to say that when you use your computer you're programming it. For example, when you sit down in front of a word processor and write a letter to your friends, you're not giving commands to the computer. You're only using the commands contained in the program. It's the computer program—which was written by a programmer—that actually tells the computer what to do.

A Computer Program

Did you ever build a model airplane? When you opened the box, you found a list of numbered instructions. By following the instructions in the order in which they were presented, you put your model together piece by piece. When you finally reached the final instruction, your model was complete.

A computer program is much like that list of instructions, except the instructions in a computer program tell the computer what to do. A computer program is nothing more than a list of commands. The computer follows these commands, one by one, until it reaches the end of the program.

Each line in a computer program is usually a single command that the computer must obey. Each command does a very small task, such as printing a name on-screen or adding two numbers. When you put hundreds, thousands, or even hundreds of thousands of these commands together,

your computer can do things like balance a checkbook, print a document, draw pictures, or blast invading aliens from the sky.

Programming Languages

Computers don't understand English and, in fact, they can't even understand the C programming language. Computers understand only one thing, machine language, which is entirely composed of numeric values. Unfortunately, human minds don't deal well with numbers.

Computers understand only numbers, right? C programs use words and symbols so people can understand the program. How, then, can the computer understand and run the program? The truth is, before you can run a C program, you must compile it.

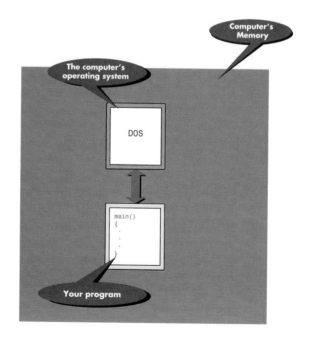

> **WHAT DOES IT MEAN?**
>
> A *compiler* changes your program into an executable file than can be understood by the computer. Some languages are compiler-based, some are not. Almost all implementations of the C programming language use a compiler.

There are all kinds of computer languages, including Pascal, C, C++, FORTRAN, COBOL, Modula-2, and BASIC. All computer languages have one thing in common: they can be read by humans. Some languages, such as BASIC, convert a program to machine language one line at a time as the program runs. Other languages, such as C and Pascal, use a compiler to convert the entire program before any of the program runs. All programming languages must be converted to machine language for the computer to understand the program.

> **WHAT DOES IT MEAN?**
>
> An *interpreter* is a program that changes programs into machine language that the computer can understand. An interpreter, such as Microsoft's QBasic, translates a program as it is executing. This is different than a compiler, which translates the code before executing the program.

The Programming Process

Writing a computer program, though not particularly difficult, can be a long and tedious process. It's much like writing a term paper for school or a financial report for your boss. You start out with a basic idea of what you want to do and write a first draft. After reading over the draft, you go back to finalize the paper until it is flawless. Over the course of the writing process, you can write many drafts before you're satisfied with the document you have produced.

Writing a program requires development steps similar to those you use when writing a paper or report. Most of the steps in the programming process are repeated over and over as errors are discovered and corrected. Even experienced programmers seldom write programs that are error-free. Programmers spend more time fine-tuning their programs than they do initially writing them.

This fine-tuning is important because we humans are not as logical as we like to think. Moreover, our minds are incapable of remembering every detail required to make a program run perfectly. Only when a program crashes or does something else unexpected can we hope to find errors that exist in programs.

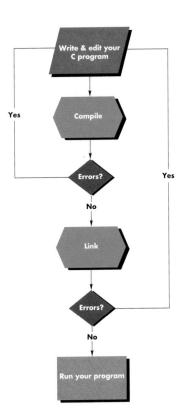

LESSON 4
Include Files

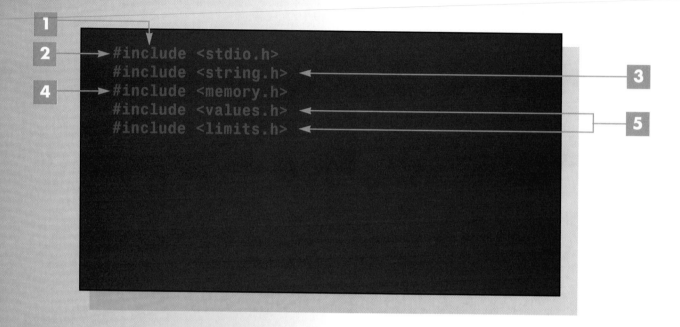

```
#include <stdio.h>
#include <string.h>
#include <memory.h>
#include <values.h>
#include <limits.h>
```

Before you can write any program in C, you have to understand the concept of include files. An *include file* is a file outside of your program that is included in your program. The include file contains functions, definitions, symbols, and a plethora of other statements that are used by your program. Many run-time library routines use constants, type definitions, or macros defined in an include file. To use the routine, you must include the file containing the needed definition(s).

WHAT DOES IT MEAN?

The *C Run-Time Library* is a set of functions that enables you to interact with the computer's memory, with the disk, with the screen, or with printers. The libraries are simply code that you can call from a C program to perform operations.

1 Include Statement

The #include directive tells the compiler that it should insert the contents of the file noted in brackets. The code from that file is literally inserted into your program to provide your program with the symbols and functions that it requires to operate.

2 Standard Input and Output

The stdio.h include file provides a set of functions for input and output on your computer. Input involves the retrieval of information from, for example, your keyboard, while output involves the display of information on your screen or printer.

With the functions available in this file, you can read a string of text that you enter from the keyboard and place that string on your screen.

Word processors use the functions in this library to enable you to enter documents and have these documents printed.

Another set of operations supported by the functions available in `stdio.h` is the one that enables you to save information to your hard drive or floppy disk. These functions are used to take information from your computer's memory, save it to a file, and load that information back into memory from a file.

3 String Operations

A string is merely text that you enter from the keyboard. `My name is Jim` is some text that C sees as a string. In C, strings are special cases of values stored in memory and must be treated as such. In `string.h` there are numerous functions that enable you to copy, move, concatenate, compare, and search strings of text.

4 Memory Operations

One very important capability that is provided for you is memory access and management. With `memory.h` you can move, copy, compare, combine blocks of memory, and perform operations directly on your computer's memory. These capabilities are useful when you are doing operations on memory that include, for example, copying blocks of text in a word processor using an edit/copy sequence of commands.

WHAT DOES IT MEAN?
To *concatenate* two strings means that you link the two strings together.

5 Values and Limits

In C you have limitations on the size of a number that can be stored in your computer's memory. The files `values.h` and `limits.h` provide you with the maximum and minimum limits for numeric values that are allowed by the C programming language.

Include File Differences

Pay attention to which include files you bring into your program. For some compilers, for example, the `values.h` include file does not exist, but the equivalent file is `float.h`. It all depends on how close the compiler's vendor decides to stay to the standards set aside for C compilers by the American National Standards Institute (ANSI).

Preprocessor   Reserved words   Identifiers and symbols   Strings and numbers   Comments

LESSON 5

Program Entry Point

```c
#include <stdio.h>
#include <string.h>
#include <memory.h>
#include <values.h>
#include <limits.h>

/*Simple main() definition*/
main()
{
    /*program-statements*/
}


/*Argument main() definition*/
main( int argc, char *argv[ ], char *envp[ ] )
{
    /*program-statements*/
}
```

All programs written in C have what is called a main() definition. This definition is the main entry point into the program and tells the computer where to begin execution of the program. main() provides a common entry point for the computer to take the commands that you enter into your program and execute them in the order specified.

1 Include Files

When you compile a program, the computer includes the files noted in the brackets next to the #include directive.

2 The Simple main() Definition

When the compiler takes the C code and converts it to the numbers that the computer understands, it takes the main() definition and prepares it for use by the computer. This is the format of main() used throughout this book.

The simple main() definition is called by the computer on startup without passing any values to the program. All that happens here is that the computer locates main() and begins execution of the program code from that point on to the end of the program.

3 Program Statements

These are the statements that are executed by the computer after it locates the `main()` definition. Each program statement located between the brackets of `main()` is executed in the sequence entered by you when you write the program.

4 Argument `main()` Definition

This `main()` definition is used when you want your program to receive information from the computer when the program is run. Such information, or values, could refer to a startup file or parameters on how the program should operate in the computer.

You may have already used programs that have this type of `main()` definition. For example, the archive program PKZIP requires you to enter the name of the zip file and some parameters to archive files. Other programs, like compilers, require the entry of the name of the program that you want to compile, along with some additional parameters.

When you run a program with the argument `main()` definition, the DOS command line looks something like this :

```
C:>diskcopy a: b:
```

In the preceding example, you see the DOS prompt, C:>, on the far left. The program, `diskcopy`, is a standard DOS program to copy disks from one drive to another. In this example, you pass the drive from which you wish to copy, `a:`, and the drive to copy to, `b:`. The parameters are `a:` and `b:` and are passed to the argument `main()` definition when the program `diskcopy` is started by the computer. The program then takes those values and uses them in the program statements to know where to copy the files on the disks.

WHAT DOES IT MEAN?

The *disk operating system* or *DOS*, is the environment that runs on a PC to control the interactions of the computer with the user. It is the brain, so to speak, of the computer, and enables you to print to a printer, write to the screen, and save and load files on a disk. All programs that you write talk to DOS in order to perform operations in the computer.

LESSON 6

Declarations

```
#include <stdio.h>
#include <string.h>
#include <memory.h>
#include <values.h>
#include <limits.h>

main()              /*Simple main() definition*/
{
    int       Variable1;
    char      Variable2;

    /*program-statements*/
}
```

A *declaration* is a statement in C that tells the computer the program needs to use a block of memory for the storage of information. All declarations have a label, otherwise known as a variable, associated with them, that is used to manage the information in a particular block of memory.

1 Include Files

When you compile a program, the computer includes the files noted in the brackets next to the #include directive.

2 Program Entry Point

The main() definition is called by the computer on startup and begins execution of the program code from that point on to the end.

3 Declarations

In the sample code, you tell the computer to allocate memory for two variables. The program tells the computer how much memory is required for each of the data types. Once allocated, the computer tells the program where the memory for the declared variables is located.

In this code you are declaring two variables. The text int and char on the left defines the types to be declared. C has many *data types* such as these. The int is an integer data type while char is a character data type.

The text to the right, Variable1 and Variable2, are the labels associated with the data types. These labels, or variable names, provide a way for you to access the integer and the character without knowing the location in memory where the information is stored.

All declarations appear at the beginning of a block of code, such as `main()`. The program has to tell the computer to allocate the memory before you can access it and use it in your program.

The main rule to remember about naming a variable is that the names cannot exceed 32 characters in length! The other important point to remember is that of case-sensitivity. The C compiler can tell the difference between variables declared with uppercase letters and those with lowercase. For instance, the variables Abc, ABC, and aBC are all different to the compiler.

4 Program Statements

These are the statements that are executed by the computer after it locates the `main()` definition. The statements use the declarations of the program for storage and manipulation of information in the computer.

LESSON 7

Function Calls

```
#include <stdio.h>
#include <string.h>
#include <memory.h>
#include <values.h>
#include <limits.h>

main()              /*Simple main() definition*/
{
    int         Variable1;
    char        Variable2;

    function_name(Variable1,Variable2);

    /*program-statements*/
}
```

A *function call* is a program statement that executes a block of code. This block of code consists of a series of additional program statements that are isolated from the rest of the program. Most of the run-time library functions are written to give you a certain capability within the computer. For example, you can call a function that copies blocks of memory or writes data to the screen. All that you see is one line of code—the function call—but inside of that function call are many lines of code to execute the actual operation of the function call.

1 Include Files

When you compile a program, the computer includes the files noted in the brackets next to the #include directive.

2 Program Entry Point

The main() definition is called by the computer on startup and begins execution of the program code from that point on to the end.

3 Declarations

The program tells the computer to allocate memory for two variables. The first variable, Variable1, is an integer and the second, Variable2, is a character.

4 Function Calls

The statement function_name(Variable1, Variable2); tells the computer to run a function named function_name. The computer looks in memory for this name and, once located, passes the variables Variable1 and Variable2 to it to begin its processing.

A function is like a small program within your `main()`. The computer only accesses the block of code within the function whenever a call is made to it within `main()`. The code inside of the function is executed in the sequence in which they are entered.

If you write a housecleaning program, the function in `main()` might be called `CleanLivingRoom`, `CleanBedroom`, `CleanKitchen`, and `CleanBathroom`. The `CleanLivingRoom` function would contain all the steps needed to clean the living room, the `CleanBedroom` function would contain all the steps needed to clean a bedroom, and so on.

Remember case-sensitivity for variables? The C compiler can also tell the difference between functions declared with uppercase letters and those with lowercase.

5 Program Statements

All function calls are part of the program statements of a program. The function calls and other statements are all called in the sequence that they are entered into the program.

LESSON 8

Commenting Your Code and Style

```c
/*Include standard files for use within the program*/
#include <stdio.h>
#include <string.h>
#include <memory.h>
#include <values.h>
#include <limits.h>

/*Simple main() definition*/
main()
{
    /*Declare a variable. for storage of the person's age*/
    int     Age;

    /*Ask the user to enter their age*/
    printf("Enter your age : ");

    /*Read in the age and store in the variable Age*/
    scanf("%d",&Age);

    /*Output the age entered by the user that is stored in
      Age*/
    printf("You are %d years old\n",Age);
}
```

1

2

3

4

5

Always comment your code! Always make sure that you can read your code and have an explanation of what is happening throughout. Many programmers develop a very cryptic style to thwart attacking program predators, while others actually provide information as to how the program works. When you create definitions within your program, make sure that you use words that are clear and understandable. When you make comments in your code, always tell the reader what is going on in the code in as much detail as required. Comments do not increase the size of your final program, and they help when you come back in six months to perform maintenance on your program or if someone else works with your code.

1 Include Statement

The `#include` statement tells the compiler that the named files should be included into the code. Notice the comment line `/*Include standard files for use within the program*/`. All comments are preceded by a `/*` and end in a `*/`. This tells the compiler the text in between is not to be compiled, but is only a comment.

2 Program Entry Point

The `main()` statement is the program's entry point and it tells the C compiler where execution begins.

3 Declarations

The program tells the computer to allocate a variable, `Age`, of the integer data type. This variable is used to store information that you enter from the keyboard. Notice that the variable name is exactly what is stored in it—an `Age`. Try to make sure your variable names are named after their data to make it easier to trace.

Notice how the declarations and all lines below are indented by a few spaces. This helps to delineate blocks of code and makes the code more readable.

4 Data Entry

The program tells the computer to accept input from you and store it into a variable. Notice the comments explaining the operations on the line immediately preceding the function calls.

The program is printing the message `Enter your age :` to the screen. The program then tells the computer to wait for you to enter your age so that it can store the value into `Age`.

5 Output

The comments, once again, describe the operation of the code immediately following. The program is, at this point, simply printing a message to the screen containing the age you entered into the `Age` variable.

Compiling and Linking

After all of the code is entered into a program, you have to perform two basic steps to get it ready to run on a computer. The first step is to compile the C code into a format known as object code. *Object code* is a numeric representation of the C code that you entered into your program. This representation is set up in numbers and symbols that tell the computer how to execute the commands that you entered. The next step is to link your program's object code. When you link the object code, you are attaching header information to the object code that tells the computer how it is supposed to load and run the object code.

From your point of view, with most compilers, all you have to do is hit a button and the C compiler takes the C code and compiles and links it for you. The figure shown is the Borland C++ 4.0 compiler compiling the program from the previous lesson. Notice how, during the compile stage, the compiler shows you the filenames it is compiling as well as the current line numbers on which it is working. At the bottom of the window, the compiler is telling you the number of warnings and errors it has encountered. These errors and warnings are the small discrepancies that you have to fix whenever you write a program to make the program fully operational.

Compiling

When a compiler compiles your code, it performs a couple of different operations. Each operation converts your code to bring it closer to being machine readable object code.

The first step is that the compiler brings in all include files. Your main program is placed into memory first. The compiler then looks at each #include directive and brings the file that is named into memory with your code.

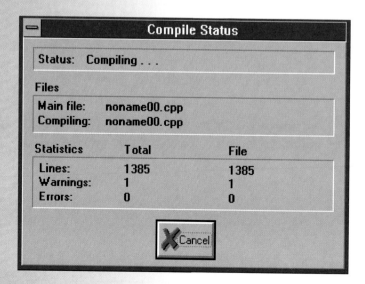

The compiler then goes through your code and replaces definitions and macros with the operational code. In most programs, definitions and macros are placeholders within a program for code. This enables you to create a piece of code once, then, with the macro or definition, mark where the code is to reside. The compiler then replaces each such macro and definition with the code it represents.

Now that all of the code is prepared, the compiler makes another pass through the code. It makes sure that the syntax of all of the statements is correct and that all variables and functions referenced within the code exist.

For now, the compiler takes the C language and converts it to object code. It reads each statement from your code and turns it into symbols and numbers storing the translated information into a file.

Linking

Once compiled, the object code can now be linked. The *linker* reads in the object code and associates all function calls to functions that exist in the C run-time libraries.

The linker locates a function called `memcpy()`, for example, in your program's object code and goes to the C run-time library. The linker attempts to locate the function in the library and, if found, tells the object code where in the library the actual code for `memcpy()` exists.

After all functions and symbols have associated references to the run-time library, the linker attaches a header to the beginning of the file. This header contains information about the program for the computer.

When you run the program, the computer reads the header and loads the program. The computer then makes a call to `main()` and your program begins executing your commands in the computer.

> **WHAT DOES IT MEAN?**
>
> The *syntax* of a program can be compared to the grammar of a language. C has a particular syntax that must be observed when writing code in the language. For example, to ask a computer "Is A equal to B?" you would ask if (A==B). Just as the question must be grammatically correct for us, the same question must have proper syntax for the computer.

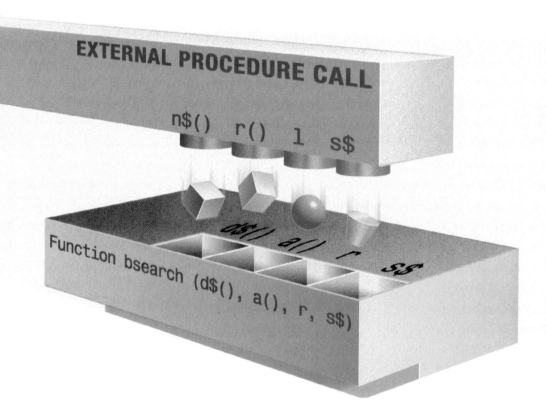

PART 3

Data Types

Data typing is a very important part of C's method of handling information. As an example, let's look at the kind of car you drive. You know that a car can take you to and from work but the type of work car you have is determined by the work you do. A pickup is used for construction, an economy car for city driving, a luxury car for the boss. If there were not so many different types of cars for different jobs—we would all have the same kind of car and have to adapt it ourselves for the job at hand.

C looks at data in much the same way. The computer sees data as merely information located in memory—no meaning, no particular format. Before your program can use that information, it has to know the type of information that is stored in memory. C's data typing allows you to use the information, that is otherwise meaningless to the computer. Without knowing the type of information stored in memory—a program can really do nothing with it, but C gives you methods of knowing what is stored in memory as well as using that information for the job at hand.

When a computer stores data in memory, that data appears as simple bytes of information in no particular format. When a program retrieves that data for processing of any type, that program has to retrieve it in such a way that the data is understandable. There needs to be a way to determine how to manipulate the data stored in memory.

Part 3: Data Types

For instance, an integer is stored in two bytes of memory while a character is stored in only one. Somehow the computer has to know how to retrieve and handle the two byte integer or the one byte character for appropriate use by your program. C data types include integers, characters, floating point numbers, and some data types defined by the user. The compiler acts differently on each type and performs actions based on the type of data stored in memory.

WHAT DOES IT MEAN?

A *byte* is a small piece of the computer's memory used to represent pieces of information. A byte can represent numeric values and characters of the alphabet. All of C's data types are made up of multiple bytes of memory.

As shown in this figure, each data type has a different size, and range of values—therefore requiring a different method of handling by the computer. The basic data types shown here are int, float, and char.

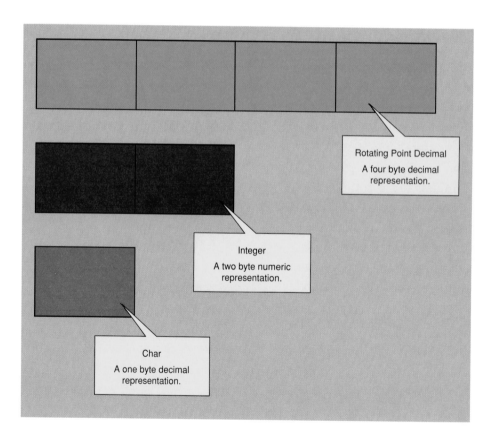

Rotating Point Decimal
A four byte decimal representation.

Integer
A two byte numeric representation.

Char
A one byte decimal representation.

Schizophrenia in C

Occasionally there is the need to make one data type look like another. To be more specific, you sometimes have to force a value into a data type that may not be defined for that type of value. The action of making one data type look like another is called *typecasting*. Typecasting in C provides a method for conversion of the type of a value. For example, if you make an entry into your program from the keyboard, your program stores the entry as a character. To perform some type of mathematical operations on the entry, you have to convert that character into an integer. Typecasting can be used to convert the character entered into the keyboard into the integer used for the mathematical operation.

User Defined Types

You can also create your own data types that are based on the standard C data types. This functionality provides flexibility in the C language so that you can customize variables needed for your particular application.

In C you can create your own data types, also known as user data types, which are merely variations of the basic `int`, `float`, `char`, and `double` data types. You also can create structures of data consisting of the fundamental data types in C—including the `int`, `float`, and `char` data types. One of these structures consists of a contiguous list of one of the C data types and is known as an *array*. The other structure consists of a combination of any of the C data types and is known, simply, as a *structure*.

LESSON 10

Integers

```c
#include <stdio.h>
#include <limits.h>

main()
{
    int     IntegerVariable;

    printf("The number of bytes in an integer
        is %d\n", sizeof(IntegerVariable));
    printf("The maximum value is %d while the
        minimum value is %d \n",
    INT_MAX, INT_MIN);
    }
```

The integer data type is used a lot in the C language for simple storage during the execution of a program. It is a numeric data type that provides for the storage of numbers. An unsigned int can range from 0 to 65,535 while a signed int, which is also the default for int, can range from–32,768 and +32,767.

WHY WORRY?

Occasionally you will have to break lines of code to fit onto a printed page, fit into your visible window, or fit within the boundaries of a compiler's established line width. These widths vary between 80, 132, and 256 characters across. The best place to break lines of code is at commas.

1 Declarations

For this program you only need one test variable of the int data type. The program declares the variable and the computer reserves 2 bytes of memory for IntegerVariable.

The int data type, as defined here, is a 2 byte data type that allows for the storage of numeric values ranging from –32,768 to +32,767. All variables declared to have the characteristics of the int data type are used in mathematical operations such as addition, subtraction, and multiplication.

WHAT DOES IT MEAN?

A *prototype* is a function definition that is used by the compiler to determine what parameters are required by the function as it is called in your program.

Other definitions for int include signed and unsigned. An unsigned int stores values in the range of 0 to 65,535 and is available strictly for non-negative numbers. A signed int, also the default for the int variable defined here, has the same range as an int and is used for applications such as checkbook managers where negative numbers abound.

The int data type cannot support remainders, such as decimals generated in division operations. They are solely for the storage of whole numbers.

2 Output

The output at this program section provides insight into the characteristics of the integer data type. The first printf() function prints the integer size using the sizeof() macro. The macro looks at the variable's data type and determines the number of bytes of that the data type uses.

The format string, text between the quotation marks, contains a text label and a format specifier. The text label provides output to the computer screen to identify the data. The %d is a *format specifier* that allows you to insert an int value into the output string. The \n is a carriage return line feed—similar to pressing the Enter key—placed in the output string to move the cursor to the next line after it prints to the screen. The value of the variable IntegerVariable is placed into the %d of the format string.

The second printf() statement prints the integer data type's minimum and maximum values. The definitions INT_MAX and INT_MIN are located in the limits.h include file and represent the maximum and minimum values allowed for an integer data type.

Like the previous printf(), the first %d prints the value of INT_MAX as an integer inserted into the format string while the second %d prints INT_MIN.

WHAT DOES IT MEAN?

A *macro* is a special type of routine and is called like a function. A macro provides a method of writing small segments of code that do not warrant writing a completely separate function.

LESSON 11
Short

```c
#include <stdio.h>
#include <limits.h>

main()
{
    short       ShortVariable;

    printf("The number of bytes in a short is
        %d\n",
        sizeof(ShortVariable));
    printf("The maximum value is %d while the
        minimum value is %d \n",
        INT_MAX, INT_MIN);
}
```

The short data type is similar to an integer but is used for porting considerations between different platforms. C is supposed to be a portable language, however, due to the characteristics of different computers the data types behave differently. For example, on one machine the int is a 2 byte data type and on others it is a 4 byte data type. The short takes care of these minor incompatibilities by maintaining a 2 byte size on different computers.

1 Include Statement

The #include statement tells the compiler that the named files should be included into the code.

2 Program Entry Point

The main() statement is the program's entry point and tells the C compiler where execution begins.

3 Declarations

For this program, you only need to declare one short variable named ShortVariable. The computer marks a 2 byte block of memory for use by the variable.

The short data type, as defined in this program, is a 2 byte data type that allows for the storage of numeric values ranging from −32,768 to +32,767. All variables that are declared to have the characteristics of the short data type are used primarily in mathematical operations such as addition, subtraction, and multiplication.

Other definitions for short include signed and unsigned. An unsigned short can store values in the range of 0 to 65,535 and is available strictly for non-negative numbers. A signed short (also the default for short as defined in this program) has the same range as a short.

As with the int data type, short cannot support decimal values.

4 Output

The first printf() function prints the size of the variable defined as a short data type using the sizeof() macro. Because the short is the same size as an int on most low-end PCs the output of this statement and of an int is identical.

The format string contains a text label and a format specifier. The text label provides output to the computer screen to identify the data. The %d is called a format specifier that allows you to insert a short int value into the output string. The \n is a carriage return line feed, similar to hitting the Enter key on the keyboard, that is placed in the output string to move the cursor to the next line. The value of the variable ShortVariable is placed into the %d of the format string for output to the screen.

The second printf() statement prints the minimum and maximum values for the integer data type. The definitions INT_MAX and INT_MIN are located in the limits.h file and represent the maximum and minimum values allowed for an integer data type.

In this printf(), the first %d prints the value of INT_MAX as an integer inserted into the format string while the second %d prints INT_MIN.

LESSON 12

Long

```c
#include <stdio.h>
#include <limits.h>

main()
{
    long      LongVariable;

    printf("The number of bytes in a long is
            %d\n", sizeof(LongVariable));
    printf("The maximum value is %ld while the
            minimum value is %ld \n",
            LONG_MAX, LONG_MIN);
}
```

The long data type is part of the integer family but allows for the storage of much larger values than the int data type. The data type unsigned long has a range of 0 to 4,294,967,295 while a signed long has the range –2,147,483,648 to 2,147,483,647. As with the int data type, the default for a long is signed.

1 Include Statement

The #include statement tells the compiler that the named files should be included in the code.

2 Program Entry Point

The main() statement is the program's entry point and tells the C compiler where execution begins.

3 Declarations

For this program, you declare one long variable named LongVariable. The computer marks a 4 byte block of memory for a long as opposed to a 2 byte block for an int.

The long data type, as defined in this program, is a 4 byte data type that allows for the storage of numeric values ranging from –2,147,483,648 to +2,147,483,647. All variables that are declared to have the characteristics of the `long` data type are used primarily in mathematical operations such as addition, subtraction, and multiplication.

Other definitions for `long` include `signed` and `unsigned`. An `unsigned long` can store values in the range of 0 to 4,294,967,295 and is available strictly for non-negative numbers. A `signed long`, also the default for `long` as defined in this program, has the same range as a `long`.

Just like the `int` and the `short`, the `long` does not support decimal values. This data type is intended for situations that require the storage of values that are much larger than can be stored in an `int` or `short` data type.

4 Output

The first `printf()` function prints the size of the `long` using the `sizeof()` macro.

The second `printf()` statement prints the minimum and maximum values for the `long` data type. The definitions `LONG_MAX` and `LONG_MIN` are located in the `limits.h` file and represent the maximum and minimum values allowed for a `long` data type.

The reason for the two separate output statements used in these programs is to provide a method for output of both the size of the data types, and the ranges for the data types. The first output statement, `printf()`, provides a method for output of the number of bytes that the computer allocates for the data type in memory using the `sizeof()` macro. The second line prints the maximum and minimum values, as defined in `limits.h` for the default `signed long`, to the screen.

LESSON 13

Float

```c
#include <stdio.h>
#include <values.h>

main()
{
    float       FloatVariable;

    printf("The number of bytes in a float is
        %d\n", sizeof(FloatVariable));
    printf("The maximum value is %g while the
        minimum value is %g \n",
        MAXFLOAT, MINFLOAT);
}
```

1

2

3

4

The float data type is one of the real number data types provided in the C language. The float data type has a range of $3.4 * 10^{-38}$ to $3.4 * 10^{+38}$.

1 Include Statement

The #include statement tells the compiler that the named files should be included into the code. Notice that here there is a new include file introduced called values.h. This file provides values for real number data types.

2 Program Entry Point

The main() statement is the program's entry point and tells the C compiler where execution begins.

3 Declarations

In the code, the program tells the computer that it is declaring one float variable named FloatVariable. The computer marks a 4 byte block of memory for a variable of the float data type.

The `float` data type, as defined in this program, is a 2 byte data type that allows for the storage of numeric values ranging from $-3.4 * 10^{-38}$ to $3.4 * 10^{+38}$. All variables that are declared to have the characteristics of the `float` data type are used primarily in mathematical operations such as division.

One of the differences to note between the previous data types mentioned and the `float` is that the `float` has a decimal portion that contains the remainder portion of a division operation as a decimal value.

4 Output

The first `printf()` function prints the size of the float using the `sizeof()` macro.

The second `printf()` statement prints the minimum and maximum values for the float data type. The definitions `MAXFLOAT` and `MINFLOAT` are located in the `values.h` file and represent the maximum and minimum values allowed for a `float` data type.

LESSON 14

Double

```
1   #include <stdio.h>
    #include <values.h>

2   main()
    {
3       double     DoubleVariable;

        printf("The number of bytes in a double is
            %d\n", sizeof(DoubleVariable));
4       printf("The maximum value is %g while the
            minimum value is %g \n",
            MAXDOUBLE, MINDOUBLE);
    }
```

The double data type is another one of the real number data types provided in the C language. The double data type has a range of $1.7 * 10^{-308}$ to $1.7 * 10^{+308}$.

1 Include Statement

The #include statement tells the compiler that the named files should be included into the code.

2 Program Entry Point

The main() statement is the program's entry point and tells the C compiler where execution begins.

3 Declarations

A double variable named DoubleVariable is declared. The computer marks an 8 byte block of memory for a variable of the double data type.

The double data type, as defined in this program, is a 4 byte data type that allows for the storage of numeric values ranging from $-1.7 * 10^{-308}$ to $1.7 * 10^{+308}$. All variables that are

44

declared to have the characteristics of the `double` data type are used primarily in mathematical operations such as division for values much larger than those that can be stored in the `float` data type.

4 Output

The first `printf()` function prints the size of the `double` using the `sizeof()` macro.

The second `printf()` statement prints the minimum and maximum values for the `float` data type. The definitions MAXDOUBLE and MINDOUBLE are located in the `values.h` file and represent the maximum and minimum values allowed for a `double` data type.

Characters

```
#include <stdio.h>
#include <limits.h>

main()
{
    char        CharVariable;
    int            x;

    printf("The number of bytes in a char is
       %d\n", sizeof(CharVariable));
    printf("The maximum value is %d while the
       minimum value is %d \n",
          CHAR_MAX, CHAR_MIN);

    for(x=0;x<=255;x++)
    {
        CharVariable = (char)x;
        printf("%c ",CharVariable);
    }
}
```

1 2 3 4 5 6

The char data type consists of a single byte and is used to store ASCII characters. The signed char data type ranges from –128 to 127 while the unsigned char ranges from 0 to 255. The values for the unsigned char are used to store the ASCII character equivalent values.

WHAT DOES IT MEAN?

An *ASCII* (pronounced *askey*) character is one that conforms to a set of standards set forth by the American Standard Code for Information Interchange. The characters are standard alphabet, number, and a few additional control characters and symbols.

1 Program Entry Point

The main() statement is the program's entry point and tells the C compiler where execution begins.

2 Declarations

The program's declaration section has one char variable named CharVariable and one int variable called x. The compiler marks a 1 byte block of memory for a variable of the char data type and a 2 byte block of memory for the int.

The char data type, as defined here, is a 1 byte data type that allows for the storage of numeric values and alphabetic characters. This data type ranges from 0 to 255 when `unsigned` and –128 to +127 when the default of `signed` is used. A variable declared to have the characteristics of a `char` stores alphabetic characters as well as small numeric values between the ranges given above.

Multiple variables are defined in this declaration section. You can define multiple variables for use with your code. You can have variables defined for each of the different data types (multiple definitions for each data type if required) for as many variables as your program requires.

3 Output

The first `printf()` function prints the `char` size using the `sizeof()` macro.

The second `printf()` statement prints the minimum and maximum values for the `char` data type. The definitions `CHAR_MAX` and `CHAR_MIN` are located in the `limits.h` file and represent the maximum and minimum values allowed for an `char` data type.

4 ASCII Character Output

The program performs a loop through all the ASCII characters and prints them to the screen. The `for()` statement tells the computer to loop through the bracketed code as many as 255 times. The `int` variable `x` stores the current loop count from 0 to 255. Looping is discussed later, but for now pay close attention to the use of the `char` data type.

5 Assignment

As the computer loops through the code, it uses the value stored in the `x` variable and assigns it to the `CharVariable`. This includes typecasting to convert the integer to a character. The value is converted from an `int` to a `char` and stored in the memory marked for `CharVariable`.

In `CharVariable = (char)x`, the casting operation occurs through the `(char)` statement. The data type you want to typecast to is placed in parentheses before the variable you want to convert. In this case `x` is an `int` you want to convert to a `char`. The statement takes the value in `x` and, when passed through the `(char)`, is converted to a `char` and stored in `CharVariable` as a `char`.

> **WHAT DOES IT MEAN?**
>
> Typecasting provides a method for conversion of one data type to another using the equal sign. You can convert a `char` data type to an `int` and vice versa.

6 Output

The next `printf()` statement prints the ASCII character stored in `CharVariable`.

LESSON 16
Strings

```
#include <stdio.h>

main()
{
    char          String[20];

    printf("The number of bytes in String
        is %d\n", sizeof(String));
}
```

Now that you know what the basic C data types are and how they are used, some user-defined data types will be discussed. A *string* is not a standard data type but can be created using a contiguous series of chars.

1 Include Statement

The #include statement tells the compiler that the named files should be included into the code.

2 Program Entry Point

The main() statement is the program's entry point and tells the C compiler where execution begins.

3 Declarations

You are declaring a string consisting of 20 characters for use in storing ASCII characters that make up a string. The computer takes this declaration and marks a block of memory 20 bytes long for the variable named String.

When declaring strings it is advisable to declare a string variable at least one character larger than you think will be required. The reason for this excess declaration is to take into account the null terminator required by a string. If you do not account for this terminator, your strings may exceed the declared size of your variable and overwrite other variables and code in the computer's memory.

4 Output

The `printf()` function prints the size of the string using the `sizeof()` macro. The macro looks at the number of bytes of the `char` data type that make up the `String` variable.

NOTE

Because a string is a series of characters, some method has to be provided to determine the end of the string. In C, a null character, which is a numeric value of zero, is placed at the end of the string. The null terminator is also represented by a \0 just as the carriage return line feed. This termination is called a *null termination* and the string is termed an *ASCIIZ string*.

LESSON 17

Pointers

```
1    #include <stdio.h>

2    main()
     {
3        int      *TestPointer;

4        *TestPointer = 100;

5        printf("The value of the pointer is %d.
           The address of the pointer is %ld",
              *TestPointer,TestPointer);
     }
```

Up till now you have seen variables in their simplest form—simple variable names of specific data types representing a block of memory for storage of information. *Pointers* look at the storage of information but not in the block of memory reserved for a variable. The pointer is not for the storage of information, but is used for referencing other memory where information is stored. The variables discussed so far are defined and given memory to use for the storage of information throughout their lifetime. The pointer can change what part of memory looked at and can point to a block of memory reserved for other variables to change or extract information. A pointer is a nonintrusive look into the memory of the computer by simply accessing different addresses of the memory.

WHAT DOES IT MEAN?

An *address* is a specific location in the computer's memory. A computer's memory is addressed consecutively with each byte having a unique address within the memory.

The primary purpose for pointers is to allow access to one block of memory by many different functions within your program. Instead of passing the value, you are passing the address of the information.

1 Include Statement

The #include statement tells the compiler the named files should be included into the code.

2 Program Entry Point

The main() statement is the program's entry point and tells the C compiler where execution begins.

3 Declarations

To declare a pointer to a particular data type, simply place an asterisk immediately before the variable name. In this case, the declaration statement is `int *TestPointer` to create a pointer to an integer data type. When you use this pointer you are accessing an `int` data type at the address pointed to by the pointer.

4 Assignment

Here you set the value of the address pointed to by `*TestPointer` to a value of 100. Notice the asterisk preceding the variable name. This asterisk performs a *dereference* to tell the computer to use the address stored by the variable and set the `int` data type at that address to the value of 100.

The value stored in a pointer is the address of a piece of information stored elsewhere in the computer's memory. When you dereference a pointer, you are telling the computer to go to the address pointed to by the pointer and, in this example, set the value stored at that address.

5 Output

The `printf()` statement prints the message `The value of the pointer is 100`. The address of the pointer is 35730183. The value of `100` is printed by dereferencing the pointer with `*TestPointer` while `TestPointer` returns the actual address where the value of `100` is stored.

When you run this program you might notice that the value 35730183 is different on your machine. This value varies depending on your computer, your operating system, and the other programs that might be running on your computer at the time. Each time you run a program, the program may reside in a different portion of your computer's memory than it did the last time you ran it. So when you look at the addresses for the pointers used in this example in your own computer, they may be different because the program may reside in a different part of memory.

WHY WORRY?

If you do not dereference a pointer when assigning or reading values you will be accessing the address of the data referenced by the pointer and not the data itself. Be especially careful when assigning values to a pointer so as not to change the address by accident. For instance, a `Pointer = 10` statement causes the pointer to reference memory address 10 while `*Pointer = 10` changes the value at the address pointed to by the pointer.

LESSON 18

Structures

```
1   struct TempStruct
2   {
        int     Integer;
3       float   Float;
        char    String[20];
    };

4   struct TempStruct       TestStruct;
```

So now that you have an understanding of the basic C data types, let's look at one of the things you can do with these data types. To go a little beyond the basic declarations, let's look at a user defined data type called a *structure*.

1 Structure Definition

The keyword struct tells the compiler that the name TempStruct is to be assigned to the combination of data types that follow the keyword between the curly brackets in the code listing. The compiler treats this structure as a unique data type consisting of each individual data type in its definition.

2 Structure Delimiters

You have seen curly brackets { } used in other ways within a program but the use of them here has a special meaning. The *members* of the structure exist between the curly brackets that mark the beginning and end of the structure, respectively.

3 Structure Members

The members of a structure define its characteristics. Each member is a variable, as you have seen before, of any standard or user-defined data type. The members are accessible like a variable, but are specific to that structure.

4 Declaration

As with any other standard or defined C data type, you must declare a variable of the data type before you can use it in your program. To declare a variable of the defined structure data type you must begin the declaration statement with the keyword `struct`.

The next word in the statement is the name of the structure for which you are creating a variable—the structure name `TempStruct`. This method of declaring structures allows you to create numerous structures for many different purposes for your program and create a new variable for each structure.

The name `TempStruct` was chosen for this example only, but any name can be used that you find suitable for the structure. Such names include `Personnel` for a structure that might manage names and addresses of people in your company or `Birthday` to maintain a structure for coworkers' birthdays.

The final word in the statement is the name of the variable that is to be used to access the structure—`TestStruct`. As with any other variable, the computer marks a block of memory large enough to hold the data for the structure. You know that an integer is 2 bytes, a float is 4 bytes, and you can see that the String variable is 20 bytes. To accommodate the entire structure, the computer marks a block of memory 26 bytes long for the variable `TestStruct`.

LESSON 19

Arrays

```c
#include <stdio.h>

main()
{
    int      IntArray[3];

    IntArray[0] = 10;
    IntArray[1] = 20;
    IntArray[2] = 30;

    printf("The array contains : %d, %d, %d\n",
           IntArray[0],IntArray[1],IntArray[2]);
}
```

1
2
3
4
5

Believe it or not, you have already been introduced to arrays when you were introduced to the user defined string data type. Similar to a structure, an *array* is a combination of data types, however, all of the data types are the same. Each of the data types within an array are accessible by referencing an element offset. To understand an array, think of a grocery list. Each entry in the list tells you something different that you have to buy but they are all groceries that have to be purchased. An array is nothing more than a list of similar elements.

1 Include Statement

The `#include` statement tells the compiler that the named files should be included into the code.

2 Program Entry Point

The `main()` statement is the program's entry point and tells the C compiler where execution begins.

3 Declarations

You are declaring an array of `int` variables for this program. Notice that the basic declaration is identical to declaring a simple variable of type `int` except that the declaration is followed by `[3]`. This tells the compiler that there are three distinct variables in this array. The offset starts at 0 to access the first integer, 1 for the second, and 2 for the third and last integer.

Because there are three integers for this structure, the computer marks 6 contiguous bytes of memory as each integer uses 2 bytes each.

4 Assignment

When you assign values to the integers of the array you must access each element separately. To place 10 into the first integer's marked block of memory access offset 0. Each consecutive integer of the array is accessed with consecutive offset values.

5 Output

To view the contents of the array use the `printf()` statement. The program prints the message `The array contains : 10, 20, 30`. Each consecutive element of the array is accessed and the contents are displayed on the screen.

WHY WORRY?

When you define an array, you tell the compiler how many elements are in that array during its declaration. For example, `int X[3]`, tells me that there are 3 integers in array X. You must always access the first element of an array at offset 0, X[0], and the last, in this example, is 2, X[2].

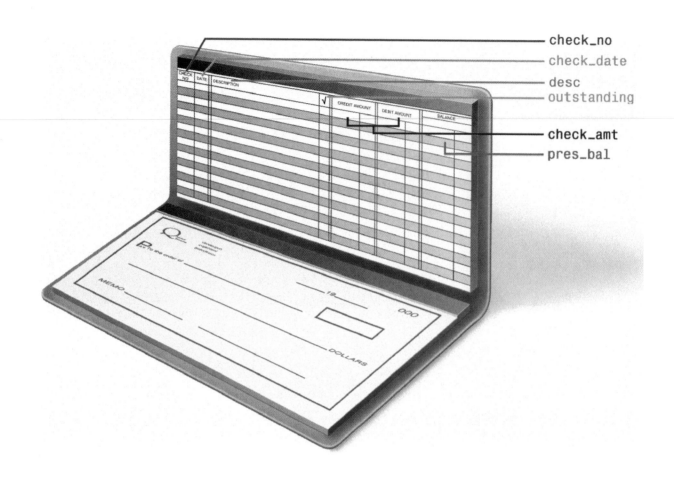

check_no
check_date
desc
outstanding

check_amt
pres_bal

|← x=2 →|

Quantity 14

x=14

PART 4

Variables and Constants

Everyone needs some level of order, some means of organizing themselves and storing their belongings, papers, bills, and so on. Let's say that you have just finished paying your bills this month and you need to file your utility bill stub. How do you do this? You walk over to your filing cabinet, open the drawer, locate the utility file folder, slide in the utility bill stub, and simply close the drawer. Now you know exactly where the utility bill stub is and have immediate access to it.

Variables

Computers maintain an order similar to your filing cabinet by storing information in blocks of memory that can be thought of as folders in a file drawer. Each block of memory contains data that is used by a program and easily can be accessed by going to that block of memory and accessing the data. Just like when you go back to the file drawer to get that utility bill and locate the file labeled "utilities," computers access blocks of memory through labeled folders or *variables*.

Variables are placeholders that mark a block of memory reserved for the storage and manipulation of information. As the name implies, you can vary the contents of memory represented by the variable.

When you enter, or store, information in your computer, your program tells the computer into which variable the information is to be placed. The computer then takes the information, locates the variable in memory, and places the information in that marked block of memory.

The figure below shows how variables are stored and accessed in a computer's memory. As you can see, each variable marks a place in memory for information storage. When you want to retrieve that information to change or delete it you can get it by calling to that variable.

Variables, as dynamic storage elements of a program, can be changed anytime during the execution of your program. There are circumstances, however, when you may want to define a variable that does not change. This reference value is constant throughout the lifetime of the program. For example, you can store the current interest rate for a loan processing application.

Constants

A variable that does not change is called a *constant*. A constant is a storage element that stores data much like a variable, but as the name implies, the data cannot be altered during the execution of your program.

As with variables, the computer accesses the block of memory marked by the constant. When the constant is declared, the computer reserves a block of memory for its use. After a value is assigned to the constant that value cannot be changed.

Computer's Memory

Variables

intvariable

floatvariable

charvariable

```
main()
{
    int    intvariable;
    float  floatvariable
    char   charvariable;
    .
    .
    .
}
```

Your program

Why would you want to use constants in your program? Occasionally you might find that a particular value is represented many times in an application. This value could be the current interest rate in an amortization program or a value representing the current population of your city. In your program you would, as common sense dictates, simply go through your program and manually enter the rate or population in each line that requires it.

WHY WORRY?

If you do attempt to set the value of a constant outside of the program's declaration section the compiler will return an error message notifying you that you cannot set the value of a constant.

Why not place a constant containing the interest rate or population in your program and use that constant throughout your code? Now when you have to change the rate or the population, simply change the constant, compile, link, and run. In this manner you change the one entry for the rate and population and have the compiler change each representation of the value throughout your code.

Another way of declaring a constant value used in your program is to use the `#define` directive. This directive allows you to assign a name to a value and use that name in your program's code to represent that value. When you compile your program the `#define` name is replaced by the literal value assigned to it.

Type Definitions

In certain circumstances, you might need to derive a data type from C's base data types and create a variable of that type. The `typedef` keyword defines a synonym for the specified type declaration and allows you to use that synonym throughout your program as a standard C data type.

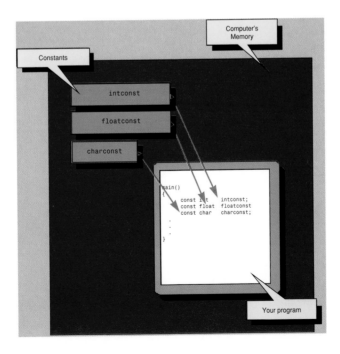

LESSON 20

Variables

```c
#include <stdio.h>

main()
{
    int        IntegerVariable;
    float      FloatVariable;
    char       CharacterVariable;

    IntegerVariable = 2;
    FloatVariable = 3.2;
    CharacterVariable = 'A';

    printf("Int : %d    Char :  %c    Float : %f\n",
        IntegerVariable, CharacterVariable, FloatVariable);
}
```

1 → `#include <stdio.h>`

2 → `main()`

3 → `float      FloatVariable;`

4 → `FloatVariable = 3.2;`

5 → `printf("Int : %d    Char :  %c    Float : %f\n",`

Now that you have a grasp on what a variable is, take a look at the following program. The program declares a few variables, sets their values, and prints the variables' values to the screen. Be sure to focus on the variable declarations and understand their usage.

1 Include Statement

The `#include` statement tells the compiler that the named file should be included into the code. The contents of this file provides keywords and function prototypes for your program to use.

WHAT DOES IT MEAN?

A *keyword* is a word that is part of the programming language. The keyword, also known as a *reserved word*, has special meaning to the compiler and cannot be used in any other way in a program.

2 Program Entry Point

The `main()` statement is the program's entry point and tells the C compiler where execution begins.

3 Declarations

At this point, focus on the declarations of the variables in the small program. Notice that there are three variables being declared, each with a different type. These variables are given a block of memory with characteristics that suit the needs of the declared type.

For example, the `int` variable, `IntegerVariable`, is given a two byte block of memory. Because the compiler knows the type of data, the size, and the location, at runtime that information is acted on accordingly by your program. The same applies to the other variables declared as `char` and `float`.

The `CharacterVariable` is a one byte `char` data type and is given one byte of memory by the computer when the program is executed. The `FloatVariable`, being declared as a `float` data type, is given two bytes of memory by the computer when executed.

4 Assignments

After the declarations for the program are concluded, the variables can be used. In this program you are assigning values to the variables. The `int` is assigned a value of 2, the `float` a value of 3.2, and the `char` the letter "a."

As these values are being assigned, the computer knows the locations of memory for the variables listed in the declaration section. At this point, the computer takes the values assigned to the variables and stores "the values in the memory reserved for each variable.

Values may be assigned to variables in a few different ways. The most prominent means of assigning values to variables is with the equal sign (=). When the computer recognizes the equal sign, it takes the value to the right of the sign and assigns it to the variable on the left.

5 Output

Now that the variables have data, you can manipulate this data or simply print it to the screen—as done here. Notice that the variables are placed into a function called `printf()`. This function, which is discussed later, takes the variables and gets the values from the blocks of memory reserved for the variables `IntegerVariable`, `FloatVariable`, and `CharacterVariable`.

LESSON 21

Constants

```c
#include <stdio.h>
main()
{
    const int      ConstantInt = 1;
    const float    ConstantFloat = 2.21;
    const char     ConstantChar = 'a';
    int            TestInt;
    float          TestFloat;
    char           TestChar;

    TestInt = ConstantInt + 1;
    TestChar = ConstantChar;
    TestFloat = ConstantFloat + 1.0;

    printf("Int : %d  Char : %c  Float : %f\n",
        TestInt, TestChar,TestFloat);
}
```

Let's use the following program to demonstrate the use of constants. To use some of the things you have already learned, some variables are included to show how variables and constants can be used together.

1 Include Statement

The `#include` statement tells the compiler that the named file should be included into the code. The contents of this file provides keywords and function prototypes for your program to use.

2 Program Entry Point

The `main()` statement is the program's entry point and tells the C compiler where execution begins. All C programs are accessed through this statement and execute the functions immediately following until the program execution halts.

3 Declarations

The declarations here differ from that of the variable declarations. For a constant, you simply precede the variable declaration with the `const` keyword to turn a variable into a constant.

`ConstantInt` is an `int` constant and is initialized to a value of 1. When a constant is initialized, the value to which it is initialized is placed into the block of memory for the constant. This value remains there for the lifetime of the constant—as long as the program is running.

The other two constants `ConstantFloat`, which is a `float` data type, and `ConstantChar`, which is a `char` data type, are initialized to 2.21 and the letter "a" respectively. These values, as with `ConstantInt`, remain in the blocks of memory for the constants as long as the program is running.

To add a little variety to the program, the last three lines define three variables, `TestInt`, `TestFloat`, and `TestChar`. These variables demonstrate the application of constants in a program.

4 Assignments

The constant's assignments are a little different from that of the variable. Notice that you are not setting the value of the constants, but are instead using the constants to set the values of the variables.

For this program the integer variable `TestInt` is set equal to the value of the constant `ConstantInt` plus 1. The `TestChar` variable is set equal to the `ConstantChar` constant, and the `TestFloat` variable equal to the `ConstantFloat` plus 1.0.

In this example, when a constant is used as part of an assignment, the computer reads the value stored at the constant's reserved memory block. The computer then adds the values for the integer and float and copies the contents to the memory block of the variable. For the character, the constant character value is merely copied to the variable character's memory block.

5 Output

Now that the variables have data, you can print their values to the screen. Notice that the variables `TestInt`, `TestFloat`, and `TestChar` are placed into a function called `printf()`. This function takes the variables and gets the values assigned to these variables from the computer's memory and prints them to the screen as part of a message.

Defining Values—
The #define Directive

```
1  #include <stdio>

2  main()
   {
3      #define      VAL1        10
       int      TestInt;

4      TestInt = 20  + VAL1;

5      printf("Integer variable added with #define Val1 = %d\n",
           TestInt);
   }
```

To take the idea of variables and constants a little further, let's take a look at the #define directive and how it applies to a simple C program.

1 Include Statement

The #include statement tells the compiler that the named file should be included into the code. The contents of this file provide keywords and function prototypes for your program to use.

2 Program Entry Point

The main() statement is the program's entry point and tells the C compiler where execution begins. All C programs are accessed through this statement and execute the functions immediately following until the program execution halts.

3 Declarations

The `#define VAL1 10` statement defines a value (`10`) with a representative name (`VAL1`). This name provides a common calling mechanism for the value it represents throughout the program. When the compiler compiles the program, it replaces each instance of the defined name with the actual value that the name represents. The advantages of using `#define` statements are that they allow you to define a value once in your program and use that value throughout your program. The compiler takes care of distributing the value throughout the program.

To store values generated during the execution of the program, the variable `TestInt` is declared. During the program's execution, the computer marks a two byte block of memory for the `TestInt` variable. When the program is running and information is assigned to the variable `TestInt`, as in `TestInt = 20`, the computer locates the block of memory for `TestInt` and places the value of 20 into `TestInt`'s memory.

4 Assignments

The assignment section of this program uses the variable `TestInt` declared in the declaration section. The literal value of 20 is added to the defined value of the `#define` statement. During compilation the compiler replaces `VAL1` with the literal value of `10`. The result of the addition is stored in the `TestInt` variable.

5 Declarations

The output section of the program uses the `printf()` statement to output the contents of the variable `TestInt`. The program first prints the message `Integer variable added with #define Val1 =` followed by the computed value stored in the variable `TestInt`.

User Defined Data Types and Variables

```
1  →#include <stdio.h>

2  →main()
   {
3      →typedef int NewInt;
4      →NewInt      TestInt;

5      →TestInt = 20;

6      →printf("TestInt, type NewInt, is %d bytes long and a
              value of %d \n", sizeof(TestInt),TestInt);
   }
```

Occasionally you need to define new data types and create variables of these types for your program. Following is a program that creates a variable of a new data type based on the int.

1 Include Statement

The #include statement tells the compiler that the named file should be included into the code.

2 Program Entry Point

The main() statement is the program's entry point and tells the C compiler where execution begins.

Lesson 23: User Defined Data Types and Variables

3 Type Definitions

The `typedef` keyword allows you to create new types based on C data types. These new data types can be used to declare variables used throughout your program. The new data types can be any combination of standard C data types or user defined data types.

The program defines a new data type called `NewInt`, which has a basic definition data type of `int`. After the definition has been established, all variables that you declare within your program maintain the characteristics of the new data type. In this case, all such declarations result in `NewInt` variables—originally an `int`.

Okay, so this seems redundant. Why not just use the basic `int` data type instead of creating a `NewInt`? This example merely demonstrates how to use the `typedef` keyword, however, you will find such definitions do occur. For example, you will occasionally find `unsigned int` data types redefined to `WORD` data types. The reason is that a `WORD`, in the computer science world, consists of two bytes and does not support signed values. Therefore, some software developers use a `typedef` to define the `unsigned int` as the `WORD` data type.

> ### WHAT DOES IT MEAN?
>
> A *user defined data type* is any data type that is not a standard C data type. Sometimes you will need to create new data types that consist of combinations of C data types to support the needs of an application. A Christmas card list—the names and addresses of your friends and family is an example. The structure is a new data type.

4 Declarations

The variable `TestInt` is declared as a data type `NewInt` to use in the program. The computer determines the base type of the `NewInt` data type and marks memory for use by the variable `TestInt`. In this instance, the marked block of memory is the same as for that of an `int` data type.

5 Assignments

The program assigns a value of `20` to the variable `TestInt`. The computer takes this value and locates the memory marked for the variable, then stores the value in that block of memory.

6 Output

The program prints the message `TestInt, type NewInt, is 2 bytes long and a value of 20` to the screen telling you the size and contents of the variable.

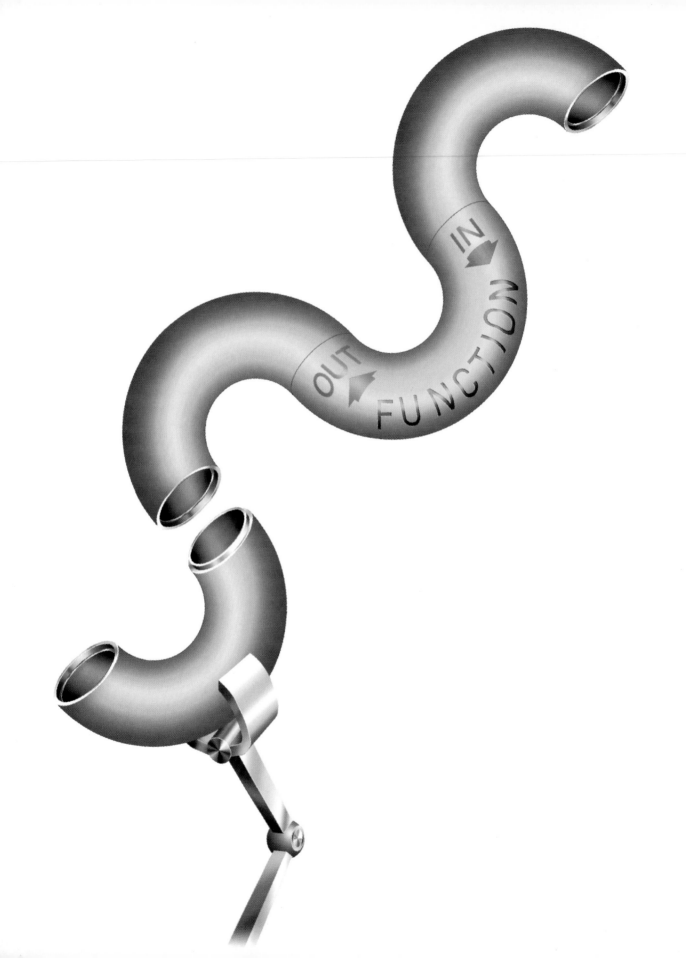

PART 5

Functions and Macros

From the examples you have seen thus far, you know how simple programs are written and operate. Most of the time you have a `main()` function containing code that is executed by the computer. But these are simple programs—what happens if you want to write something much more complex? Are you going to simply stuff hundreds of lines of code between the curly brackets of the `main()` function? Or is there a better way to handle the development of large programs.

Functions

As a matter of fact there is a better way to handle the development of large programs! When you are developing large programs, take a modular approach. The first advantage to this method is that it gives you a chance to verify that each discrete operation of the program executes properly. Another advantage to the modular approach is readability—if *you* can't read the code and follow it, who is going to maintain it? *Functions* are the answer. A *function* is a callable module of code and looks much like the `main()` function with which you are familiar. The difference between `main()` and a regular function is that the regular function is called from within the `main()` function. Modularity comes into play when you encapsulate certain operations within a function.

Each function performs a specific task, but, in conjunction with other functions, adds to the features and functions of the overall program. When you develop an application you can break it into parts. Each part, or function, has a certain operation that it can perform. When many different, but related, functions are placed together, much like a puzzle, you have a fully functional, but modular, application.

Another important point involved in the development of modular applications is *information hiding*. This may sound like an odd term for programming principles, but it is a very important issue. The idea of information hiding deals with the fact that discrete components of an operation are hidden from the rest of the program. For example, suppose you write a small function that adds two numbers together and returns the result. When you go to use this function, all you really need to know is how to call this function because the actual addition operation is internal to that function. The actual implementation of this function is hidden and primarily unimportant to the rest of the program. The only visible information for the function is the calling mechanism, the parameters, and the return values.

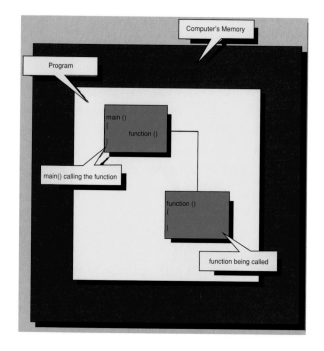

Macros

A *macro* is more or less a cousin of the function because it too is callable and contains code. The difference lies in how the macro is handled within a program. A function establishes a specific place in memory when the computer runs your program. To access the features of the function, the program simply jumps to the address of the function to execute the code of the function and returns to the previous segment of code when the function completes.

A macro is a bit backward in that regard. Instead of jumping to an address, the compiler literally places the code for the macro wherever a reference to the macro exists within your program. By making the code inline to the program's code, the execution is actually more efficient because the computer doesn't have to jump around looking for functions.

WHAT DOES IT MEAN?

An *inline statement* is replaced with the complete code it represents. All inline code, such as a macro, is written to encapsulate certain discrete operations such as adding two numbers, or getting a character from the screen.

So how do you know when it is necessary to use a macro or a function? This decision is more or less up to you when you develop your application. If your code segment is nothing more than a single line that contains no function calls, then it might be good to use a macro. If the code segment is large or you make function calls within it, create a function. One thing to remember is that the code for a macro is copied throughout your program wherever the macro is referenced, so you won't want a 200-line macro duplicated throughout your program. A macro this length can make your compiled and linked code a bit on the overbearing side for the computer. In such a case, use a function whose code exists once and is called when its segment of code is needed.

Now let's take a look at how to create functions and macros as well as how they work. Functions and macros are very important parts of the C language. Mastering the lessons in this section will establish an excellent base of understanding for the remainder of this book as well as the C programming language. The one thing to remember is that every call you make in C is either a function or a macro.

LESSON 24

Functions and Function Prototypes

```c
#include <stdio.h>
void      print_word(char *string);

main()
{
    char      WordString[20];
    printf("Enter a word to print : ");
    scanf("%s",WordString);
    print_word(WordString);
}

void      print_word(char *string)
{
    printf("The word is : '%s'\n",string);
}
```

1 — void   print_word(char *string);

2 — char   WordString[20];

3 — printf("Enter a word to print : ");
scanf("%s",WordString);

4 — print_word(WordString);

5 — void   print_word(char *string)
{
}

A function allows you to encapsulate code into discrete operational blocks. Almost every bit of code that you are going to write will have a call to one of C's functions. The files that you include into your C programs contain what are known as *prototypes*. Each of these prototypes provides a function's definition and parameters.

WHAT DOES IT MEAN?

A *parameter* is any value or variable that is passed to a function. Parameters are located between parentheses next to a function name and provide a means of sending information between the main() function and other functions of a program.

1 Function Prototype

The function prototype provides a definition for the function print_word(). Without the prototype, the C compiler sees the function call in main() before the function itself. This causes the compiler to generate an error because it doesn't know any function called print_word(). The prototype tells the compiler that the function does indeed exist, as well as the parameters to be passed to the function. This allows the compiler to continue compilation and place all code for the prototyped function into the block of memory reserved by the prototype.

The one parameter to be passed to the function, defined by the proto-type, is a string. The `char *` is a pointer to a string of characters that are passed to the function. In this program, the pointer contains the address of and points to the string contained in the variable `WordString`. When the function receives the pointer, it is able to read the information in `WordString`'s block of memory by going to that address referenced in the pointer `string` located in the function's parameter.

Notice the `void` reference preceding the function name. This tells the computer that the function does not return any values after it has completed its execution. This is covered in a more detail in the next lesson.

2 Declarations

In this program, you are only declaring one string variable, `WordString`. It stores the string to be printed.

3 Data Entry

The program tells the computer to print the message `Enter a word to print :` to the screen using the `printf()` function. The program then waits for you to enter a string and press the enter key. The `scanf()` function then stores the string you enter into the variable `WordString`.

4 Function Call

The program calls the function `print_word()`. Notice that the variable `WordString` is placed in parentheses following the function call. This is where parameters are passed to functions so that the function can receive data it is given.

5 Function Definition

The function definition is the actual block of code that contains the function name, parameter definitions, and functional code. When the function is called, it reads the information passed to it in the `char *string` pointer. The pointer itself references the variable `WordString` from the `main()` function. The function calls `printf()` to print the message `The word is :` followed by the string that was entered in `main()`.

Function Return Values

```
#include <stdio.h>
1   int      CalcSum(int Val1, int Val2);

    main()
    {
         int      IntVal1;
         int      IntVal2;
         int      RetVal;

2        printf("Enter the first number to add: ") ;
         scanf("%d",&IntVal1);
         printf("Enter the second number to add: ") ;
         scanf("%d",&IntVal2);

3        RetVal = CalcSum(IntVal1,IntVal2);
4        printf("The sum of %d and %d is %d\n",
                 IntVal1,IntVal2,RetVal);
    }

    int      CalcSum(int Val1, int Val2)
    {
5        int      Val;

         Val = Val1 + Val2;
         return(Val);
    }
```

Now that you understand the basics of functions, let's move on and see what happens with a function that returns a value to its caller. In general terms, the *caller* is any function, or the `main()` function, that tells the program to jump to the address of the defined function and execute the code located there.

1 Function Prototype

This defines a function called `CalcSum()` that takes two numbers, adds them, and returns the sum. Notice that there is an `int` instead of a `void` preceding the function name. The `int` data type tells the compiler that the function returns an integer value.

2 Declarations

The program uses the `printf()` function to request the entry of two values to be added together. The computer prints these to the screen and waits with the `scanf()` function until you enter the requested values. The `scanf()` function reads the values you enter and stores them in the variables `IntVal1` and `IntVal2`.

Notice the `&` operator preceding each of the variables in the `scanf()` function. The ampersand (`&`) tells the compiler to place the value being entered at the address of the variable listed—pass by reference. When the compiler places the entered value at the address of the variable, the value becomes visible to all functions of the program, not just to the `scanf()` function. Using this method, the `scanf()` function is able to send the integer you entered back to `main()` for use in the rest of the program.

3 Function Call

The program makes a call to the function `CalcSum()` passing the numeric values of the two variables that you just entered at the `scanf()`s. Notice the `RetVal =` preceding the call to the function. The computer takes the value to be returned by the function and places it into the block of memory marked for `RetVal`.

4 Output

The program tells the computer to print a message to the screen containing the original values entered for the calculation and the sum of the two values calculated by the function `CalcSum()`. The original values are stored in `IntVal1` and `IntVal2` while the sum, returned from the function call, is stored in `RetVal`. The `printf("The sum of %d and %d is %d\n", IntVal1,IntVal2,RetVal)` function prints a message to the screen containing the values used in the calculation as well as the sum. `%d` is used as a placeholder within the format string `The sum of %d and %d is %d\n` and allows the insertion of integers into the string. The value of `IntVal1` is inserted for the first `%d` from the left, `IntVal2` in the second, and `RetVal` in the third or final `%d`.

5 Function Definition

The function definition for this function contains two `int` parameters. The `main()` function calls this `Calcsum()` function and passes to it `Val1` and `Val2`. The values are read by the function out of its local variables `Val1` and `Val2`. The function then adds the two values and stores the result in the local variable `Val`. The variable `Val` is then returned to `main()` for storage in its local variable.

> **WHAT DOES IT MEAN?**
>
> A *local variable* is a variable that only can be seen and used inside of one function. Any variable defined inside of a function is said to be local to that function and cannot be accessed by any other function .

> **WHAT DOES IT MEAN?**
>
> A *global variable* is a variable that can be seen and used in all functions. Any variable defined at the very top of a program, above the `main()` function, is said to be global to the program and can be accessed by all functions.

Functions: Parameter Passing by Value

```
        #include <stdio.h>
1  ──►  void       SetValue(int Val);
2  ──►  main()
        {
3  ──►  int        IntVal;
   ──►  int        TempVal;

4  ──►  printf("Enter a number : ");
   ──►  scanf("%d",&IntVal);

5  ──►  TempVal = IntVal;

6  ──►  SetValue(IntVal);
7  ──►  printf("Original value is %d. Set value is %d.",
                TempVal, IntVal);
        }

   ──►  void SetValue(int Val)
   ──►  {
8  ──►  Val = 100;
   ──►  printf("Inside the function the value is %d\n",Val);
   ──►  }
```

Passing a value to a function is a common method of transferring data to a function so that the function can operate on that data. In this lesson you are simply looking at the effects of changing the values of variables in a function. In previous lessons operations performed on a function were discussed, but in this lesson you learn how data gets into the function.

1 Function Prototype

This defines a function called `SetValue()` that takes a number (`Val`), attempts to change its value, then prints the result.

2 Program Entry Point

The `main ()` statement is the program's entry point and tells the C compiler where execution begins.

3 Declarations

The program is declaring two variables. `IntVal` is used to store a value that you enter. `TempVal` temporarily is set equal to the value of `IntVal` for purposes of outputting to the screen.

4 Data Entry

The program uses the `printf()` function to request the entry of the value. The `scanf()` function reads the value you enter and stores it in the variable `IntVal`.

5 Assignment

The program takes the value stored in `IntVal` and assigns it to the variable `TempVal`. The computer actually makes a copy of the value stored in `IntVal`'s marked block of memory and puts that copy in `TempVal`'s marked block of memory.

6 Function Call

The program makes a call to the function `SetValue()` passing `IntVal` as the parameter. This type of parameter passing is called *pass by value* because the actual value stored in the passed variable is copied to the function's parameter line. The value then becomes local to that function by way of its parameter.

7 Output

The computer prints a message containing the value that you entered and the value set by the function. The one thing you will notice when you run this program is that the values are identical. The reason is that any changes to variables passed by value are not visible outside the function in which the changes occurred because they are local only to that function.

8 Function Definition

The function definition takes the value copied into its parameter variable (`Val`) and sets it equal to 100. The function then prints the variable's value to show that it was indeed changed. The variable `Val` is local to the function and any changes to that variable are local. This means that the change of the variable's value to 100 is not seen in the caller (the main program, in this case).

WHAT DOES IT MEAN?

Pass by value is a method of parameter passing that copies the value of a variable into a function parameter. Variables are passed by value to functions whenever the value of the variable is not going to be changed by the function.

Preprocessor   Reserved words   Identifiers and symbols   Strings and numbers   Comments

Functions: Parameter Passing by Reference

```
#include <stdio.h>
void        SetValue(int *Val);

main()
{
    int     IntVal;
    int     TempVal;

    printf("Enter a number : ");
    scanf("%d",&IntVal);

    TempVal = IntVal;

    SetValue(&IntVal);
    printf("Original value is %d. Set value is %d.",
           TempVal, IntVal);
}

void  SetValue(int *Val)
{
    *Val = 100;
    printf("Inside the function the value is %d\n",*Val);
}
```

1

2

3

4

5

6

So now you can get the data into the function, but how do you get it back out? You know how to return values from the function but there also is another method that allows you to extract data from the function's parameter line. The method of *passing by reference* has many other uses than just returning data from a function, but this lesson concentrates on data movement. Note the subtle differences between passing by reference and passing by value, and the impact these differences have on the operation of the program.

1 Function Prototype

This defines a function called SetValue() that takes a number, changes its value, then prints the result. The asterisk, made part of the parameter for the function definition, tells the program that a pointer to an integer is passed to the function. By passing a pointer to an integer, you are telling the function the address of the integer variable IntVal. This passing by reference allows the function SetValue() to change the value of IntVal and allow main, the caller of SetValue(), to receive the new value of IntVal.

2 Data Entry

The program uses the `printf()` function to request the entry of the value. The `scanf()` function reads the value you enter and stores it in the variable `IntVal`.

3 Assignment

The program takes the value stored in `IntVal` and assigns it to the variable `TempVal`.

4 Function Call

The program makes a call to the function `SetValue()`, passing `IntVal` as the parameter. Notice the ampersand (&) preceding the variable. This operator tells the computer that it is to pass the address of the variable and not the value. This type of parameter passing is called *pass by reference* because the address of the variable is copied to the function's parameter thus referencing the variable in memory.

5 Output

The computer prints a message containing the value that you entered and the value set by the function. In this program the values are different because the variable was changed in the function.

6 Function Definition

The function definition here looks much like the ones seen in previous lessons except for the asterisk (*) preceding the variable name. The asterisk operator tells the computer that any information passed to the function by way of this parameter is an address pointing to a variable located in the calling function.

The function `SetValue()` then *dereferences* the pointer. The dereferencing operation, symbolized by the asterisk operator again, tells the computer to set the memory block pointed to by the address in `Val` to 100. The function then prints this value to the screen to show that it changed inside the function.

WHAT DOES IT MEAN?

Pass by reference is a method of parameter passing that copies the address of a variable into a function parameter instead of the value of the variable. A variable is passed by reference to a function whenever the variable is to be changed by the function. The address of the changed variable is then sent back to the previous segment of code, the calling code, for use in the rest of the program.

WHAT DOES IT MEAN?

Dereferencing is the method of accessing the block of memory pointed to by a pointer. When you dereference a pointer you are telling the computer to get the information located at the address contained in the pointer for your use.

Preprocessor   Reserved words   Identifiers and symbols   Strings and numbers   Comments

LESSON 28
Macros

```c
#include <stdio.h>

#define     VADD(X,Y) (X+Y)

main()
{
    int     IntVal1;
    int     IntVal2;

    printf("Enter the first number    : ");
    scanf("%d",&IntVal1);
    printf("Enter the second number   : ");
    scanf("%d",&IntVal2);

    printf("The sum of %d and %d is %d\n",
        IntVal1, IntVal2, VADD(IntVal1,IntVal2));
}
```

1

2

3

4

As you have seen, a function is a block of code that performs a certain operation. You may find that a function might be overkill in some instances. For example, why write a function to add the values of two variables when you can simply enter an equation such as A + B into the code to add the variables together. The solution to this dilemma is a *macro*. Let's take a look at macros, their definitions, and their use in a program.

1 Macro Definition

The VADD() macro allows you to pass two values (X and Y) to it and add them together returning a sum. Notice that the definition itself is similar to that of a function, but the code associated with the macro is a bit different. All you see is the small operation that occurs on the two values to be passed.

2 Declarations

The program is declaring two variables. `IntVal1` and `IntVal2` that are
used to store the values entered.

3 Data Entry

The program uses the `printf()` function to request the entry of the
values. The `scanf()` function reads the values you enter and stores them
in the variables `IntVal1` and `IntVal2`.

4 Output

The program prints a message to the screen containing the two values
you entered and the sum of the values calculated by the macro. The
macro is entered into the `printf()` statement and allows the results of
the addition to be printed. When you compile the program, the macro
is replaced by its code. The C compiler takes the macro definition
`VADD(X,Y)` and literally replaces it with `(X+Y)`. In this program,
`VADD(IntVal1,IntVal2)` is replaced by `IntVal1 + IntVal2`.

One advantage to using a macro is that of efficiency. The code becomes
inline allowing all operations to be directly incorporated into the code.
Another advantage is that of maintainability. Instead of going through
your code and entering numerous calculations, you can replace these
calculations with a macro. You can enter the equation into the code if
desired, but if you have this same equation in the code many times,
maintainability becomes cumbersome. With only one instance of the
equation as a macro, all you have to do is change that one defintion of
the equation and let the compiler distribute it throughout your code. The
macro allows you to maintain one instance of the calculation that is then
moved to all the places in the code that call to that macro.

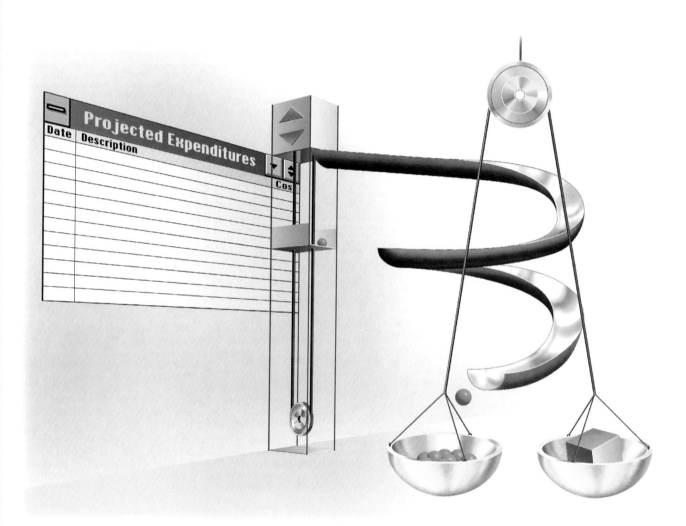

PART 6

Mathematics

You have probably heard that programming a computer requires much use of math. All those formulas and equations you learned in high school probably look like some foreign language now. Most programs require only simple mathematical calculations, such as addition, subtraction, multiplication, and division—the same calculations you use to balance your checkbook.

Math in C

When you are writing a program, you won't have to wear down pencils adding long columns of numbers nor will you get a migraine trying to divide huge numbers with long division. The computer can perform the calculations for you. If you know how to use the basic operations to solve simple problems, you know all the math necessary to write a computer program in C.

Along with learning the basic mathematical functions of C, you are introduced to a couple of advanced functions. These functions are not too difficult, but they provide you with the ability to calculate the power and square root of numbers that you provide for your program.

One thing to remember when performing calculations in C is that the language follows the standard order of operations for mathematics. If you don't pay attention to

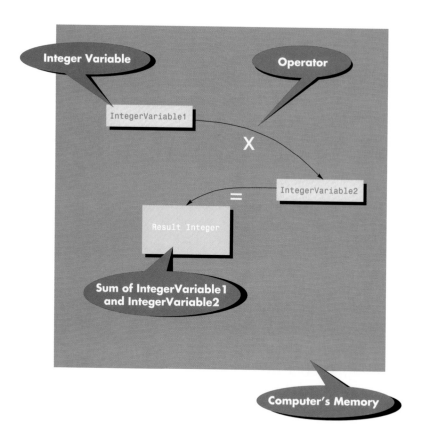

the order of operations you might come up with a result for a calculation that isn't even close to what you expected. For instance, multiplication and division are performed before addition and subtraction. So unless you are aware of this order your result may not be what you expected.

Order of Precedence

The order of operations are as follows from highest precedence to lowest. The first in the list, multiplication, always occurs first unless you surround an equation by parentheses. The equation in parentheses takes precedence as in 2 * (3 + 2). The 3 + 2 are added before multiplying by the 2. If 2 * 3 + 2, the multiplication occurs first then the addition.

(...)	Parentheses
*	Multiply
/	Divide
%	Modulus
+	Add
−	Subtract

---

do is write a program that tells the computer what has to be done and voila, it will agitate and calculate, based on your commands, for hours. In this chapter, you learn how to do just that.

You can't avoid math entirely. I tried for years to do so and ended up being a mathematician—who was to know? After all, computers are number-crunching machines that like nothing better than to sit and come up with the results of hundreds, thousands, or even millions of calculations. It's up to you to give the computer the commands it needs to perform those calculations. All you have to

LESSON 29
Multiplication

```c
#include <stdio.h>

main()
{
        int      IntegerVariable1;
        int      IntegerVariable2;
        int      MultResult;

        printf("\nEnter the first integer to multiply  :");
        scanf("%d",&IntegerVariable1);

        printf("\nEnter the second integer to multiply :");
        scanf("%d",&IntegerVariable2);

        MultResult = IntegerVariable1 * IntegerVariable2;

        printf("%d * %d = %d\n",
                IntegerVariable1,IntegerVariable2,MultResult);

        MultResult *= 2;

        printf("Doubling the result yields : %d\n",
            MultResult);
}
```

To demonstrate mathematical operations in C, let's create a small calculator that performs some basic math operations. Enter the program below into your computer to see how C handles multiplication and other operations.

1 Declarations

In this program you declare one variable for each value that you are going to multiply as well as one variable for the storage of the result. IntegerVariable1 holds the first value, while IntegerVariable2 holds the second variable.

The variable MultResult stores the result of the multiplication operation. The computer allocates 2 bytes per int variable to store the numbers.

2 Entry of Values

Before you can perform the multiplication operation, you must enter the values to be multiplied. The printf() function prints a message to the screen requesting values to be entered. The scanf() function actually reads the values that you enter and stores them in the variables IntegerVariable1 and IntegerVariable2.

86

Notice the & operator preceding each of the variables in the `scanf()` function. The ampersand tells the compiler to place the value being entered at the address of the variable listed—pass by reference. This is one situation in which pointers come into play. When the compiler places the entered value at the address of the variable, the value becomes visible to all functions of the program, not just to the `scanf()` function.

> **WHAT DOES IT MEAN?**
>
> An *operator* is a special symbol in C that operates on variables. For example, the + operator can represent the addition operation.

3 Multiplication

Now that the values have been entered, you can multiply them together and come up with a result. The variables `IntegerVariable1` and `IntegerVariable2` are multiplied together. This operation occurs by placing an asterisk, *, between the values to be multiplied. The computer takes the variables' values, multiplies them together, and then places the result into `MultResult`.

4 Output

The program reads the variables and outputs the values to the screen with the multiplication equation.

5 Multiplication

Look closely at this line of code. Again you are multiplying, but now you are using a different form for the equation. In this instance, you are taking the `MultResult`, provided by the previous multiplication, and multiplying it by a value of 2. This result is then placed back into `MultResult`.

This additional form of multiplication is used if you are performing a single operation on a variable such as in `MultResult`. In this example, you are multiplying `MultResult` by 2 using `MultResult*=2`. Another way of showing this is `MultResult = MultResult *2`. So, which way is best? In the long run it is up to the programmer. While `MultResult*=2` is much more efficient, performing less operations in the computer to multiply the variable by 2, the second form, `MultResult = MultResult *2`, is much more readable.

6 Output

Once again there is output that shows the contents of the `MultResult` variable. The output value is equal to twice the value produced in the previous output.

Preprocessor   Reserved words   Identifiers and symbols   Strings and numbers   Comments

LESSON 30
Division

```c
#include <stdio.h>

main()
{
    float    FloatVariable1;
    float    FloatVariable2;
    float    DivResult;

    printf("\nEnter the numerator    :");
    scanf("%f",&FloatVariable1);

    printf("\nEnter the denominator :");
    scanf("%f",&FloatVariable2);

    DivResult = FloatVariable1 / FloatVariable2;

    printf("%f / %f = %f\n",
           FloatVariable1, FloatVariable2, DivResult);

    DivResult /= 2;

    printf("Halving the result yields : %f\n",DivResult);
}
```

Division in C is as simple as changing one mathematical operator in a program. The division operator, /, takes the value on the right and divides it into the value on the left.

1 Declarations

To store the values the program is going to work with, you have to declare one float type variable for the numerator, one float type variable for the denominator, and a third float type variable for the quotient. The float data type is used in the program instead of the int

data type to allow you to take the result out to several decimal places, as required.

2 Entry of Values

The printf() function prints a message requesting the entry of the numerator and the denominator for the division operation. The scanf() function reads the decimal values and stores the data in the float variables.

3 Division

Now that the values have been entered and are stored in FloatVariable1 and FloatVariable2, the computer can divide these values to provide a result. The computer takes the value for `FloatVariable2` and divides it into the value for `FloatVariable1`, placing this result into the block of memory marked for `DivResult`.

4 Output

The program reads all the variables of the program and outputs the values to the screen in the form of the division equation.

5 Division

As with multiplication, there is also another form of division that can be used. You still perform a standard division operation, but divide `DivResult` by 2 and place this result back into the block of memory marked for `DivResult`.

This additional form of division is used if you are performing a single operation on a variable as in the `DivResult` example. In this example, you are dividing `DivResult` by 2 using `DivResult/=2`. Another way of performing this division is `DivResult = DivResult / 2`. As with multiplication, the choice of which method to use is up to the programmer. While `DivResult/=2` is much more efficient, performing less operations in the computer to divide the variable by 2, the second form, `DivResult = DivResult / 2`, is much more readable.

6 Output

The output of this previous division operation is placed on-screen and shows the contents of the `DivResult` variable. This value is equal to one half the original value that was in the memory marked for `DivResult`.

Addition

```c
#include <stdio.h>

main()
{
        int     IntegerVariable1;
        int     IntegerVariable2;
        int     AddResult;

        printf("\nEnter the first value to add   :");
        scanf("%d",&IntegerVariable1);

        printf("\nEnter the second value to add  :");
        scanf("%d",&IntegerVariable2);

        AddResult = IntegerVariable1 + IntegerVariable2;

        printf("%d + %d = %d\n",
                IntegerVariable1, IntegerVariable2, AddResult);

        AddResult += 10;

        printf("Adding 10 to the result yields : %\n",
            AddResult);
}
```

The addition operator, +, adds the value on the left of the operator to the value on the right. In this lesson you use the calculator from the multiplication and division lessons to make an addition calculator.

1 Declarations

In this calculator program you define two integer variables, IntegerVariable1 and IntegerVariable2, for use in storing the values you want to add together. A third integer variable, AddResult, is defined to store the result of the addition of IntegerVariable1 and IntegerVariable2.

2 Entry of Values

The printf() function prints a message requesting the entry of the values for the addition operation. The scanf() function reads the integer values and stores the data in the int variables.

3 Addition

The computer now takes the two entered integers and adds them together. The values stored in `IntegerVariable1` and `IntegerVariable2` are added together by the operation of the + operator. The computer takes the result of the addition operation and places this result into the `AddResult` variable's block of memory marked in the declaration section.

4 Output

The `printf()` function, `printf("%d + %d = %d\n",` `IntegerVariable1, IntegerVariable2, AddResult)`, reads `IntegerVariable1` and `IntegerVariable2` and places these values on either side of the plus sign in the format string. The function then reads `AddResult` and places its value after the equal sign. The format string, which is discussed in detail later in this book, is then printed to the screen in the form of an addition equation.

5 Addition

Once again there is a second format for the addition operation. The program takes the result of the previous addition and adds 10 to the value. The result of the addition is placed into the block of memory for `AddResult`.

This second form of addition is used if you are performing a single operation on a variable as in the `AddResult` example. In this example you are adding 10 to `AddResult` using `AddResult+=10`. Another way of performing this addition is `AddResult = AddResult + 10`.

To add a little variety to the addition function, there is one more method of addition you can use. It is in the form of the *increment* operator. This operator adds 1 to a variable and is formatted as `AddResult++`. This form adds 1 to the current value of `AddResult` just as `AddResult = AddResult +1`. This method is used whenever you only want to increment a variable by 1.

WHAT DOES IT MEAN?

The *increment* operator, `++`, adds one to a variable.

6 Output

The output of this addition operation is placed on-screen and shows the contents of the `AddResult` variable. This value is equal to the original value plus 10.

LESSON 32

Subtraction

```c
#include <stdio.h>

main()
{
    int     IntegerVariable1;
    int     IntegerVariable2;
    int     SubResult;

    printf("\nEnter the first value to subtract :");
    scanf("%d",&IntegerVariable1);

    printf("\nEnter the second value to subtract:");
    scanf("%d",&IntegerVariable2);

    SubResult = IntegerVariable1 - IntegerVariable2;

    printf("%d - %d = %d\n",
           IntegerVariable1, IntegerVariable2, SubResult);

    SubResult -= 10;

    printf("Subtracting 10 from the result yields :
           %d\n",SubResult);
}
```

The subtraction operator, -, subtracts the value to the right of the operator from the value to the left. In this lesson you modify the addition calculator to perform subtraction.

1 Declarations

In this calculator program you define two integer variables, IntegerVariable1 and IntegerVariable2, for use in storing the values you want to use in the subtraction operation and one variable, SubResult, to store the result.

2 Entry of Values

The printf() function prints a message requesting the entry of the values for the subtraction operation. The scanf() function reads the integer values and stores the data in the int variables.

3 Subtraction

The computer takes the two entered integers and subtracts IntegerVariable2 from IntegerVariable1. The values stored in IntegerVariable1 and IntegerVariable2 are subtracted by the function of the - operator.

The computer takes the result of the subtraction operation and places this result into the `SubResult` variable's block of memory marked in the declaration section.

4 Output

The program reads all the variables of the program and outputs the values to the screen in the form of the subtraction equation.

The `printf()` function, `printf("%d - %d = %d\n", IntegerVariable1, IntegerVariable2, SubResult)`, reads `IntegerVariable1` and `IntegerVariable2` and places these values on either side of the minus sign in the format string. It then reads `SubResult` and places its value after the equal sign. The format string is then printed to the screen in the form of a subtraction equation.

5 Subtraction

There is a second format for the subtraction operation. The program takes the result of the previous subtraction and subtracts `10` from the value. This result is placed into the block of memory for `SubResult`.

This second form of subtraction is used if you are performing a single operation on a variable as in the `SubResult` example. In this example, you are subtracting `10` from `SubResult` using `SubResult-=10`. Another way of performing this subtraction is `SubResult = SubResult - 10`.

A third method, as with addition, is in the form of the *decrement* operator. This operator subtracts `1` from a variable and is formatted as `SubResult--`. This form subtracts `1` from the current value of `SubResult` just as `SubResult = SubResult - 1`.

WHAT DOES IT MEAN?

The *decrement* operator, `--`, subtracts one from a variable.

6 Output

The output of this subtraction operation is placed on the screen, using the `printf()` function, showing the contents of the `SubResult` variable. This value is equal to the original value minus `10`.

LESSON 33
Modulus

```c
#include <stdio.h>

main()
{
    int     IntegerVariable1;
    int     IntegerVariable2;
    int     ModResult;

    printf("\nEnter the numerator  :");
    scanf("%d",&IntegerVariable1);

    printf("\nEnter the denominator:");
    scanf("%d",&IntegerVariable2);

    ModResult = IntegerVariable1 % IntegerVariable2;

    printf("%d %% %d = %d\n",
           IntegerVariable1, IntegerVariable2, ModResult);

    ModResult %= 10;

    printf("The remainder of dividing by 10 yields :%d",
        ModResult);
}
```

1
2
3
4
5
6

When dividing values that do not divide equally, you end up with a remainder. If you use a float data type for the storage of the division result, this remainder will be the decimal value.

1 Declarations

To calculate the modulus of two numbers, you declare two int variables to store the values entered. The IntegerVariable1 and IntegerVariable2 integer variables are given 2 bytes of memory each. A third integer variable

is ModResult which is used to store the result of the modulus operation.

2 Entry of Values

The printf() function prints a message requesting the entry of the values for the modulus operation. The scanf() function reads the values and stores the data in the int variables.

3 Modulus

The computer can now take the two entered integers and find the remainder, or modulus, of

IntegerVariable1 divided by IntegerVariable2. The values stored in
IntegerVariable1 and IntegerVariable2 are operated on by the %
operator. The computer takes the result of the modulus operation and
places this result into the ModResult variable's block of memory.

4 Output

The program reads all of the variables of the program and outputs the
values to the screen in the form of the modulus equation.

The printf() function, printf("%d %% %d = %d\n", IntegerVariable1,
IntegerVariable2, ModResult), reads IntegerVariable1 and
IntegerVariable2 and places these values on either side of the modulus
sign in the format string. It then reads ModResult and places its value after
the equal sign. The format string is then printed to the screen in the form
of a modulus equation.

5 Modulus

Another format for the modulus operation follows in line with each of
the mathematical operations presented earlier. The program takes the
result of the previous modulus and performs another modulus operation.
This time the result of ModResult and 10 are taken. The result of the
modulus is placed back into the block of memory for ModResult.

This second form of the modulus operation is used if you are performing
a single operation on a variable as in the ModResult example. In this
example you are determining the remainder of ModResult / 10. The
other way of performing this addition is ModResult = ModResult % 10.

6 Output

The output of this modulus operation is placed on the screen that shows
the contents of the ModResult variable. This value is equal to the
remainder of dividing the value in ModResult by 10.

WHAT DOES IT MEAN?

A *modulus* is the
remainder of a division
operation. For example,
in the equation $10/6$, the
result is 1 with a
remainder of 4. The
modulus in this equation
is the remainder—the
value 4.

NOTE

You might find the
modulus operation helpful
in calendar calculations
when determining leap
years. Because a leap
year occurs every fourth
year, take the modulus
of the current year
(1994) and the number
$4 - 1994/4 = 498.5$; the
resultant modulus is 2.
The modulus of a leap
year is always zero,
therefore 1994 is not a
leap year.

LESSON 34

Powers

```c
#include <stdio.h>
#include <math.h>

main()
{
    double      DoubleVariable1;
    double      DoubleVariable2;
    double      PowResult;

    printf("\nEnter the value :");
    scanf("%lf",&DoubleVariable1);

    printf("\nEnter the power    :");
    scanf("%lf",&DoubleVariable2);

    PowResult = pow(DoubleVariable1, DoubleVariable2);

    printf("%g^%g = %g\n",
            DoubleVariable1, DoubleVariable2, PowResult);

}
```

Now that you have an understanding of some of the basic mathematical operations, let's take a look at an advanced math function—pow(). This function allows you to provide a value and raise it to the power of another—for example, x^y.

1 Include Statement

The #include statement tells the compiler that the code should include the named file. Notice here that an additional file called math.h should be included. Other functions available in math.h include trigonometric functions such as cos(), sin(), and tan(), random number

generator functions, and logorithm functions. The previous math functions discussed are part of the standard library of C. After you start using advanced functions such as pow(), you have to bring in the appropriate include files that contain the prototypes, operators, and symbols for the operation.

2 Program Entry Point

The main() statement is the program's entry point and tells the C compiler where execution begins.

3 Declarations

You declare three variables of the double data type to store the values for our calculation. The variables DoubleVariable1 and DoubleVariable2 store the values you want to use to calculate the result of the pow() function. The variable PowResult is used to store the result of this function.

4 Entry of Values

The printf() function prints a message requesting the entry of the values for the pow() function. The scanf() function reads the values and stores the data in the double variables.

5 Calculating the Power

The program takes the values stored in DoubleVariable1 and DoubleVariable2 and passes them to the pow() function. The function then calculates the result by raising DoubleVariable1 to the power of DoubleVariable2. This result is placed into the memory block for PowResult.

6 Output

The program reads all of the variables of the program and outputs the values to the screen, using the printf() function, in the form of a power equation.

LESSON 35

Square Roots

```
1    #include <stdio.h>
     #include <math.h>

2    main()
     {
3        double      DoubleVariable;
         double      SqrtResult;

4        printf("\nEnter the value to calculate the square
            root :");
         scanf("%lf",&DoubleVariable);

5        SqrtResult = sqrt(DoubleVariable);

6        printf("The square root of %g is %g\n",
                 DoubleVariable, SqrtResult);

     }
```

Now that you can calculate the result of a power, let's go the other way and calculate the root. For this calculator, you use the `sqrt()` function to calculate the square root.

1 Include Statement

The `#include` statement tells the compiler that the code should include the named file. As with the `pow()` function, you have to include `math.h` because the `sqrt()` is not a simple, standard C operation but is instead a function that is defined in the runtime libraries of the C compiler.

2 Program Entry Point

The `main()` statement is the program's entry point and tells the C compiler where execution begins.

3 Declarations

You declare two variables of the `double` data type for this calculator. The variable `DoubleVariable` is used to store the values you want to use to calculate the result of the `sqrt()` function. The variable `SqrtResult` is used to store the result of this function.

4 Entry of Values

The `printf()` function prints a message requesting the entry of a value for the `sqrt()` function. The `scanf()` function reads the value and stores it in `DoubleVariable`.

5 Calculating the Square Root

The program takes the value stored in `DoubleVariable` and passes it to the `sqrt()` function. The function then calculates the result by taking the square root of `DoubleVariable`. This result is placed into the block of memory reserved for `SqrtResult` in the declaration section of the program.

6 Output

The program reads the `DoubleVariable` and `SqrtResult` of the program and outputs the values to the screen, using the `printf()` function, in a statement describing the square root equation.

PART 7

Comparing Data

Not only is a computer an excellent number crunching device but it also excels at making decisions. One of the most basic components of a computer's decision making mechanism is in its data comparison capabilities. Is value A greater than, less than, or equal to, value B, and if so what operation should be performed by the computer? By using the basic comparisons of greater than, less than, or equal to, you can create a program that makes decisions based on the information stored in the program's declared variables.

Comparison Operators

Comparison operations can be used in your programs when a user performs data entry. Occasionally the user enters invalid information and, without data validation by the computer, the data is stored and used in your program, causing the program to crash. One way around this is to stand over the user and make sure he enters the information the way it is supposed to be entered—integers into integers, floats into floats, and strings into strings.

WHAT DOES IT MEAN?

Data validation involves the verification of information entered into a computer. For example, if a user is entering birthdates into a database manager, you want to be sure that information such as December 33, 1994 is not entered. You can have the program check that the date of the birthday doesn't exceed 31 for the month of December.

The automated way around this is to check the information before it is accepted by your program and stored in its variables. Let's say that the user is asked to enter a number between 10 and 50. To discover whether a number is within this range, you must check not only that the number is greater than or equal to 10, but also that the number is less than or equal to 50. To help handle these situations, C features *relational operators*—less than (<), greater than (>), and equal to (==)—and *logical operators*—AND (&&), OR (¦¦), and NOT (!), which are used to combine expressions in an if statement. A limit operator acts upon variables to determine their relationship to one another. A logical operator works on variables to return a result based on the value of the variables in conjunction with a rational condition.

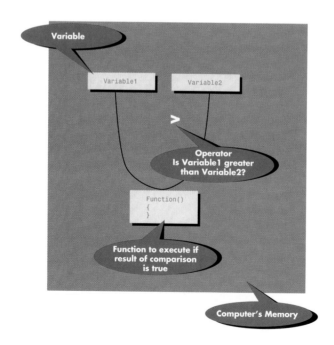

Comparison Functions

Another method of comparison used in C is memory block comparison. The program calls to a function—`memcmp()`, `strcmp()`, `strncmp()`, and `strstr()`—which tells the computer to look at the memory marked by specified variables. This method provides flexibility in the comparisons—especially when it comes to the differences in the data types.

To take this comparison section one step further, let's take a long but very brief leap into the area of artificial intelligence (AI). One specific area of AI involves the use of software called expert systems. An *expert system* is a program that makes decisions by looking at the values of variables declared in its declaration section.

For example, an expert system can be used to determine the condition of your car's engine and what might be wrong with it if your engine does not start one morning. The expert system can get the values for the voltage in your battery and the amount of gas in your gas tank and store the values in variables named `Gas` and `Voltage`. When the program gets these two values and stores them, it is performing the same operation that you do when entering the information at the keyboard. Data is being entered into the program from the car rather than from the keyboard. The expert system then looks at the statement `If Voltage > 0 && Gas ==0 then printf("You are out of gas\n")`. In this case, if the battery still has some amount of voltage and your gas tank is empty, then a message prints to the screen that tells you that you are out of gas.

This expert system example is quite simple but you can see that decisions are used in all types of programs at all levels. AI is an immense area of research and covers a lot of different areas, but it all boils down to having a computer making a decision based on the values stored in the variables of a program.

Let's take a look at a few data comparison operators and functions and see how they are used in some sample programs. Make sure to enter these programs and try them out, modify them, and play with them to get a feel for these operations and the C language.

LESSON 36

More or Less

```c
#include <stdio.h>

main()
{
    int      IntegerVariable1;
    int      IntegerVariable2;

    printf("\nEnter the first integer to compare  :");
    scanf("%d",&IntegerVariable1);

    printf("\nEnter the second integer to compare :");
    scanf("%d",&IntegerVariable2);

    if(IntegerVariable1 > IntegerVariable2)
        printf("%d is greater than %d\n",
            IntegerVariable1, IntegerVariable2);

    if(IntegerVariable1 < IntegerVariable2)
        printf("%d is less than %d\n",
            IntegerVariable1, IntegerVariable2);

    if(IntegerVariable1 == IntegerVariable2)
        printf("%d is equal to %d\n",
            IntegerVariable1, IntegerVariable2);
}
```

1

2

3

4

5

This small calculator compares values instead of performing mathematics. This program gives you an exercise in the three basic relational operators—greater than (>), less than (<), and equal to (==).

1 Declarations

To perform the comparison of two values, you declare two integer variables IntegerVariable1 and IntegerVariable2. Recall from the earlier section on data types that the computer marks 2 bytes for each of the variables in the example because they are int data types.

2 Entry of Values

The program requests that you enter a couple of numeric values on which the comparison is performed. The printf() statement prints a statement to the screen requesting that two values be entered. After each request, the `scanf()` statement takes each entered value and stores it into the block of memory marked for `IntegerVariable1` and `IntegerVariable2`.

3 Greater Than Comparison

The computer looks at the values stored in the memory marked for the variables. It then compares `IntegerVariable1` to `IntegerVariable2` to see whether `IntegerVariable1` is greater. Using the functionality of the `if` statement discussed later in this book, if the value stored in `IntegerVariable1` is greater than the value of `IntegerVariable2`, the `printf()` function immediately following is executed, outputting the results of the comparison to the screen. If the value of `IntegerVariable1` is not greater than the value of `IntegerVariable2`, the `printf()` function is not executed.

4 Less Than Comparison

The program tells the computer to compare `IntegerVariable1` and `IntegerVariable2` again. The computer checks the two values to see whether `IntegerVariable1` is less than `IntegerVariable2`. If so, the computer prints a message telling you the result of the comparison using the `printf()` function.

5 Equal To

This last statement compares the two variables to see if they are equal in value. The computer takes the value in `IntegerVariable1` and the value in `IntegerVariable2` and checks to see if they are the same. If so, the `printf()` statement prints a statement telling you so.

WHAT DOES IT MEAN?

The equality operator uses two equal signs (==), while the assignment operator uses one (=). A common mistake is to place one equal sign in a comparison, causing odd things to happen. If you use an assignment operator in a comparison, the value at the right of the operator is assigned to the value at the left—as in A=B. In this case, the values end up being equal and the comparison is true all the time.

LESSON 37
Logical Operations

```c
#include <stdio.h>

main()
{
    int        IntegerVariable1;
    int        IntegerVariable2;

    printf("\nEnter first value to compare  :");
    scanf("%d",&IntegerVariable1);

    printf("\nEnter second value to compare :");
    scanf("%d",&IntegerVariable2);

    if(IntegerVariable1 && IntegerVariable2)
        printf("%d ANDed with %d is TRUE\n",
            IntegerVariable1, IntegerVariable2);

    if(IntegerVariable1 || IntegerVariable2)
        printf("%d ORed with %d is TRUE\n",
            IntegerVariable1, IntegerVariable2);

    printf("%d NOT is %d\n",
            IntegerVariable1,!IntegerVariable1);
    printf("%d NOT is %d\n",
            IntegerVariable2,!IntegerVariable2);
}
```

Logical operations allow you to determine if a condition is true or false as opposed to comparison operations that simply determine the relation of two values to one another. The logical operators AND(&&), OR (||), and NOT (!) allow you to take two values and determine if the values are logically true or false.

1 Declarations

To perform the comparison of two values, you declare two integer variables `IntegerVariable1` and `IntegerVariable2`. These variables store the values that you enter for the logical comparison.

2 Entry of Values

The program requests that you enter a couple of numeric values on which the comparison is performed. The `printf()` statement prints a statement to the screen requesting that two values be entered. After each request, the `scanf()` statement takes the entered value and stores it into the block of memory marked for `IntegerVariable1` or `IntegerVariable2`.

3 Testing the AND Logical Operator

The computer takes the values of `IntegerVariable1` and `IntegerVariable2` and performs an AND logical comparison on them. If both of the values are equal to 1, or greater than or less than 0, the `printf()` function is executed. If either one of the values is 0, the program continues on to the next statement.

WHAT DOES IT MEAN?

The AND operator (&&) compares the values of two variables and produces a true result if the variables are both true.

4 Testing the OR Logical Operator

The computer now takes the variables' values and performs a logical OR on them. In this case, if either or both of the values are 1, or greater than or less than 0, then the `printf()` statement executes—telling you the result.

WHAT DOES IT MEAN?

The OR operator, ¦¦, compares the values of two variables and produces a true result if either of the variables is true.

5 Testing the NOT Logical Operator

The NOT operator inverts the value that it precedes. If the value of the variable it precedes is greater than or less than 0, the value is set to 0. If the value of the variable is equal to zero, the value of the variable is set to 1. This logical value flipping is important when determining if a variable is logically NOT set to a particular value. If `!A` is TRUE then the value of `A` is 0 because negating a 0 results in a 1—thus TRUE.

WHAT DOES IT MEAN?

The NOT operator, !, changes the logical value of a variable to the opposite. If a variable is true then the NOT operator changes it to false and vice versa.

LESSON 38

Comparing Blocks of Memory

```c
#include <stdio.h>
#include <string.h>

main()
{
    int       IntegerArray1[2];
    int       IntegerArray2[2];

    printf("\nEnter first array to compare  :");
    scanf("%d",&IntegerArray1[0]);
    printf("\n                    :");
    scanf("%d",&IntegerArray1[1]);

    printf("\nEnter second array to compare :");
    scanf("%d",&IntegerArray2[0]);
    printf("\n                    :");
    scanf("%d",&IntegerArray2[1]);

    if(!memcmp(IntegerArray1,IntegerArray2,
        sizeof(IntegerArray1)))
            printf("Array 1 equals Array 2\n");

}
```

1

2

3

There are occasions when you want to compare blocks of data but are unable to use logical or relational comparisons. Situations like this occur when you are looking at data types such as structures or arrays. To compare such entities, use C's memcmp() function.

1 Declarations

Remember the example in Lesson 19 covering arrays? They are used here to demonstrate the use of the memcmp() function. The program declares two arrays, IntegerArray1 and IntegerArray2, of type int for use in storing integers that you enter from the keyboard. Both of these arrays contain two int elements and are accessible by selecting the appropriate offset within the array. The intricacies of arrays will be expanded to give you more detail in Lesson 46.

2 Entry of Values

The program asks you, with the `printf()` function, to enter a couple of values to store in the arrays. As you can see, the first `printf()` prints the message `Enter first array to compare :`. The program then calls `scanf()` to wait for you to enter a number to be stored into the first member of `IntegerArray1`—`IntegerArray1[0]`.

The second `printf()` prints a carriage return/line feed, `\n`, followed by a series of spaces, followed by a colon. The only reason for the second `printf()` is to align the colon for the second request for input with the colon for the message printed by the previous `printf()`. The program then calls `scanf()` to wait for you to enter a number to be stored into the second member of `IntegerArray1`—`IntegerArray1[1]`.

3 Memory Comparison

The program executes the `memcmp()` function telling the computer that it should do a comparison of the blocks of memory marked for the two arrays. The computer performs a byte by byte comparison on the arrays. The `sizeof()` macro, as you have seen before, tells the computer exactly how many bytes it is to compare within each array.

Notice the logical NOT operator preceding the `memcmp()` function. This operator tells the computer to invert the result of the function. If the return of the function is a 0, representing a match on the arrays, the result is flipped to a 1. So what happens if you have a structure, in this case an array, to compare to another structure? There are no operators available in C that allow you to perform a comparison unless you compare each member of the structures to the others.

In this example, you can compare each of the integers in the arrays to one another with the equality operator such as `IntegerArray1[0] == IntegerArray2[0]` and `IntegerArray1[1] == IntegerArray2[1]`. This requires two lines of code. Imagine if you declared an array of 400 integers, or even 1,000! The `memcmp()` function simply compares the blocks of memory for the arrays to one another—all in one line of code!

Comparing Strings

```c
#include <stdio.h>
#include <string.h>

main()
{
    char        String1[20];
    char        String2[20];

    printf("\nEnter first string to compare  :");
    scanf("%s",String1);

    printf("\nEnter second string to compare :");
    scanf("%s",String2);

    if(!strcmp(String1,String2))
        printf("String 1 equals String 2\n");

}
```

1
2
3
4
5

Strings are unique instances of character arrays. Because they are unique they must be treated as such in the C language. The strcmp() function of C allows you to perform a case-sensitive comparison on strings up to the null terminator.

1 Include Statement

The #include statement tells the compiler that the named file should be included into the code.

2 Program Entry Point

The main() statement is the program's entry point and tells the C compiler where execution begins.

3 Declarations

The program declares two strings, String1 and String2, to allow you to store the strings you want to compare. The strings are given 20 bytes of memory each but you can actually store only 19 characters. Remember that the last character of a string is a null terminator, so at 19 characters, the 20th character is the terminator.

Recall from the previous discussions on data types that a string is an array but an array is not always a string. A string is an array of characters terminated by a null terminator, \0. When an array of characters is terminated by a null terminator, it is a string; otherwise the array is simply of an array of members of the char data type.

4 Entry of Values

The program uses the printf() function to request the entry of a couple of strings. Two strings are read in using scanf() and stored into the string variables String1 and String2.

Notice in the scanf() functions that the string variables are not preceded by an ampersand (&). The reason for this has to do with the way strings are managed in memory. A regular int, float, or char variable involves a pass by value to the function. This prohibits the value of the passed variable from being changed and seen by other functions. The ampersand preceding such variables provides a pass by reference pointer, to allow the value to be changed and visible to all. With a string, the variable is already a pointer and automatically gets passed by reference to functions like scanf().

5 String Comparison

The program executes the strcmp() function, telling the computer that it should do a comparison of the strings. The computer performs a character by character comparison on the strings. The comparison is case-sensitive, so if you have any mismatched cases in the strings, the comparison fails.

The logical NOT operator preceding the strcmp() function inverts the result of the function. If the return of the function is a 0, representing a match on the strings, the result is flipped to a 1. The value of 1, being true, then tells the if statement that it should go ahead and execute the printf() to display the results of the comparison.

WHY WORRY?

Brackets, [...], are used when declaring arrays to tell the compiler how many elements of the data type are used for the named array. For example, the declaration int IntArray[10] tells the compiler that the array IntArray has 10 int data type members.

WHY WORRY?

There are several functions available for string comparisons and most of them are case-sensitive. There are, however, equivalent functions available that provide for non-case-sensitive comparisons. In this program you use strcmp() for a case-sensitive comparison, whereas the non-case sensitive function is strcmpi().

LESSON 40

Comparing Parts of Strings

```
1   #include <stdio.h>
    #include <string.h>

2   main()
    {
3       char        String1[20];
        char        String2[20];
        int         Length;

        printf("\nEnter first string to compare   :");
        scanf("%s",String1);

        printf("\nEnter second string to compare :");
4       scanf("%s",String2);

        printf("\nEnter the number of characters to compare
            :");
        scanf("%d",&Length);

5       if(!strncmp(String1,String2,Length))
            printf("The first %d characters of String 1
                equals String 2\n", Length);

    }
```

This lesson continues to look at strings, but a little twist is added to the comparison operation. The strcmp() function compares strings up to the null terminator; however, you might want to compare only part of the string on some occasion. This partial comparison is accomplished with the strncmp() function.

1 Include Statement

The #include statement tells the compiler that the named file should be included into the code.

2 Program Entry Point

The main() statement is the program's entry point and tells the C compiler where execution begins.

3 Declarations

The program declares two strings, String1 and String2, to allow you to store the strings you want to compare. The program also declares an int variable called Length to store a value that you will enter to determine the number of characters to compare.

4 Entry of Strings

The program uses the printf() function to request the user to type in a couple of strings. The two strings are read in using scanf() and stored in the string variables String1 and String2.

5 Entry of Length

The program now tells the computer to print the message Enter the number of characters to compare : to the screen using the printf() function. The computer then waits with the scanf() function until you enter a value for the Length variable.

The Length variable is used in the program to tell the computer how many characters are to be compared in the two strings. The method of string comparison using strncmp() allows you to compare a subset of two strings for the number of characters specified in this variable Length starting at the beginning of the string.

6 String Comparison

The program executes the strncmp() function, telling the computer that it should do a comparison of the strings for the number of characters indicated by the Length variable. The computer performs a character by character comparison on the strings up to the number of characters indicated. The comparison is case-sensitive, so if you have any mismatched cases in the strings, the comparison fails.

If the return of the function is a 0, representing a match on the strings, the result is flipped to a 1 by the logical NOT operator. The TRUE value, !0 = 1, tells the if statement to execute printf() to display the results of the comparison.

WHY WORRY?

The strcmp() function is best used whenever you are comparing entire strings. A perfect example of this is if you are searching for a particular last name in database records. The strncmp() function comes into play when you are looking for everyone whose last name starts with *Smi* in a database for use in a market survey.

Preprocessor   Reserved words   Identifiers and symbols   Strings and numbers   Comments

Finding a String in a String

```c
#include <stdio.h>
#include <string.h>

main()
{
    char        String1[20] = "The quick brown fox";
    char        String2[20];
    char        *OutString;

    printf("The main string is '%s'\n",String1);

    printf("\nEnter string to search for :");
    scanf("%s",String2);

    OutString = strstr(String1,String2);

    printf("The located string is '%s'\n",OutString);
}
```

So now you know how to compare strings and compare parts of some strings, but what about locating a string within a string? On occasion you might want to search for one string inside another. Such searches are useful when you are, for example, searching for a particular word in a word processing document. There are times when you are writing a document and have to go back and find one particular word to replace it or change it. Because a word processor sees a document as a string, you can use the strstr() function to look for that specific word in the document.

1 Include Statement

The #include statement tells the compiler that the named file should be included into the code.

2 Program Entry Point

The main() statement is the program's entry point and tells the C compiler where execution begins.

3 Declarations

String1 is initialized to The quick brown fox in the declaration section. This gives the program a string on which to perform the searches. String2 is declared to store the string that you want to search for in String1. The pointer variable, `OutString`, is marked in memory by the computer to hold the address of the string that you find in `String1`.

4 Output

The program prints the message `The main string is 'The quick brown fox'` to the screen using the `printf()` function. The function takes the string `The quick brown fox` from `String1` and writes it into the format string `The main string is '%s'`. The `%s` format specifier is a placeholder for a null terminated string.

5 Entry of Search String

The `printf()` function requests that you enter a search string. The `scanf()` function reads the string that you enter and stores it into the memory marked for the string variable `String2`.

6 String Search

The comparison operation takes the string in `String2` and compares it to each consecutive substring in `String1` of the same length as `String2`. For example, if `String2` is two characters long, `strstr()` starts at the first character of `String1` and compares the first two characters of `String1` to the two characters in `String2`. If they match, the search ends right there. If they do not match, `strstr()` compares the next two characters in `String1` to the two characters in `String2`. The function `strstr()` continues through the string until it either reaches the end of `String1` or a match is found. If `strstr()` locates `String2` in `String1`, the address of the substring within `String1` is stored in the pointer `OutString`. If no match is found by the time the end of `String1` is reached, a 0 (zero) is stored in `OutString`.

7 Output

The program calls the `printf()` function to print the result of the string search stored in `OutString`. If a string was found, it is printed to the screen with the message `The located string is`. If no string was found, the message `The located string is (null)` is printed to the screen.

WHAT DOES IT MEAN?

Because `Outstring` is a pointer, it contains the address of the substring in `String1`. This address is the beginning of the substring that contains the string searched for in `String2`. Refer to Lesson 17 for an idea as to how the pointer is used in this example.

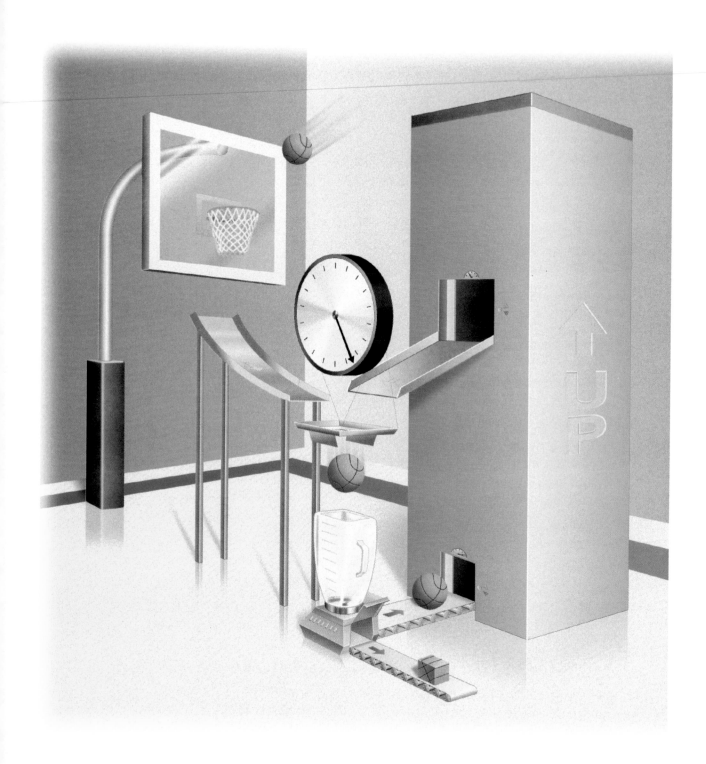

PART 8

Operations on Data

After information is stored in a computer, you can perform many operations on it. Operations like copying, moving, and converting are easily performed in the C programming language. Simply, C can access the computer's memory and manipulate information based on the commands that you enter into a program.

There are many operations you can perform on data, including mathematical operations and input/output. The operations discussed in these lessons are those that involve the actual accessing and handling of data. These operations include moving, copying, indexing, and converting.

Copying and moving data are the most widely used methods of data handling in C. The action of copying data is just as the name implies. You are taking data from one location in memory and copying it to another. The program actually handles data at a level lower than the standard data types of, for example, `int` and `char`. When doing memory copying, the program handles data at the byte level, so all data typing is transparent to the copying operation. This type of operation is useful in making backup copies of information in memory to perform some type of processing on the original without losing the data. Another area of use for this type of operation is database management. Many times it is more efficient to copy one large record than it is to copy each field of the record separately. Just imagine making one copy operation for the whole record instead of one copy operation for each field of the record.

You can use the standard memory copy operations on strings; however, strings are a special case. Strings, if you recall, are arrays of characters terminated with a null character—a null terminator. Copying blocks of memory using standard memory management functions works on strings, but C has a set of functions specific for strings. Operations such as copying and concatenating can be easily accomplished by calling functions in C. This type of operation is particularly important to text processing applications. Strings and character arrays are the basis for the operation of text processors, so the specific copying and concatenation of strings in C is quite useful.

> **WHAT DOES IT MEAN?**
>
> *Concatenation* is the process of combining two or more strings. For example, if we were to concatenate the strings "The quick" and "brown fox" the resulting string is "The quick brown fox".

Data conversion is an important part of C. Converting from one data type to another, and converting strings to numbers and back again, provide C with an immense amount of flexibility. The flexibility helps you to move data around and make the data behave the way that you want for a given application.

An important area of data conversion is called *typecasting*. Casting provides a method of taking, for example, an `int` data type and placing it into a `float` and vice versa.

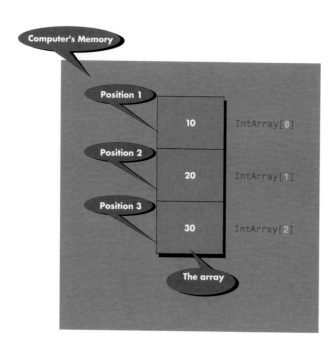

WHAT DOES IT MEAN?

Typecasting is a method of converting a value from one data type to another. When you typecast, for example, an `int` data type to a `float`, the value stored in an `int` variable is converted to and stored in a `float` variable.

Why would you want to convert information from one type to another? Occasionally, you find that certain functions require a specific data type and you don't have it handy. Your users enter an integer value into a data entry screen and your database only stores floating point decimal values. Typecast the `int`s into `float`s. A group of engineers found that it is more efficient to transmit a series of two-byte `float`s than it is to transmit a series of four-byte `double`s. Typecast the `double`s into `float`s.

Another important use of typecasting is generic data management. For simplicity, you can write many different functions to handle processing on numerous data types. To minimize coding, you can also write one function to handle many different data types. But, how do you set up this one function's parameters to accept `float`s, `int`s, `char`s, and a plethora of other data types? The answer is simple: typecast all the data types into a character array and pass it to the internals of the function by way of the function's `char` array parameter.

In line with moving, copying, and converting data, accessing the information is essential. Arrays enable you to access elements by offset. If you have an array of `int`s available to you and you want to access the fifth `int` in the array, you can simply go to that element and handle the data. These types of structures enable you to manage, for example, thousands of data elements by simply indexing to a given element instead of declaring thousands of individual variables for a similar storage.

Structures allow you to access the elements by name. If you recall, a structure can be made up of numerous data types. Each data type is marked by a name, similar to a variable. To access a member, or element, of a structure, simply call to the name of the member within that structure. This type of access helps you to keep, for example, records in a database. Each database record consists of different pieces of information, also known as fields. The structure, in a similar manner, is a record that maintains different types of information with each type of information accessible like a field in a record.

So, why do you want to know all of this? It is important that you know how C manages information and how you can use C's functions to operate on your data. Look at some of the basic operations that you can perform and see how to use C-based functions to do it easily. Don't worry—it is all really quite simple, as you will see.

LESSON 42
Copying Memory

```c
#include <stdio.h>
#include <memory.h>

main()
{
    int     Val1;
    int     Val2;

    printf("Ent<None>er a numeric value : ");
    scanf("%d",&Val1);

    memcpy(&Val2, &Val1,sizeof(int));

    printf("Value 1 is %d.  The copied value 2 is
        %d.\n", Val1, Val2);

}
```

Copying memory is merely a matter of taking one block of memory, duplicating it, and placing it into another location. C helps you to perform this operation with one simple function call along with a few pointers to memory locations containing data.

1 Include Statement

The #include statement tells the compiler that the named files should be included in the code. The include files provide prototypes for standard input and output, stdio.h, as well as memory management functions, memory.h.

2 Program Entry Point

The main() statement is the program's entry point, and it tells the C compiler where execution begins.

3 Declarations

The program tells the computer to allocate two integer variables. The variable named Val1 is used to store a value that you enter from the keyboard. The variable Val2 is used to store a copy of the value in Val1.

4 Data Entry

The program tells the computer to print the message Enter a numeric value : to the screen using the printf() function.

The program waits for you to enter a number and to press Enter. The `scanf()` function stores the number you enter into the variable `Val1`.

Notice the use of the ampersand operator in the `scanf()` function. This operator tells the computer to read the value entered at the keyboard and place it into the address where the integer variable `Val1` is located. Remember pointers back in Lesson 17? The ampersand points to the memory location (address) of the integer variable in which the entered value is stored.

Ampersand Usage

You do not use an ampersand when the variables to be copied are already pointers—as discussed in Lesson 17. Because you are making a change to the variables passed to the `memcpy()` function, you have to tell this function where in memory the variables are located. If the variables are not pointers, they must be preceded by an ampersand.

---

5 Copying Memory

The `memcpy()` function (whose prototype is located in `memory.h`) is called to copy memory you specify. The variable `Val2` is passed to the function as the destination of the data to be copied. `Val1` is the origin and contains the number that was entered into the `scanf()` function.

Notice that each of the variables is preceded by an ampersand. This operator tells the function `memcpy()` to use the addresses of the variables passed—just like in the `scanf()` function. The `memcpy()` function copies the data out of the address of `Val1` then stores the data into the address of `Val2`. The first parameter of the function is always the destination of the copy operation, and the second is always the source. The third parameter of the function tells how many bytes are to be copied from the address of `Val1` to the address of `Val2`. In this instance, an `int` is only two bytes long, so the third parameter is equal to 2—as retrieved with the `sizeof()` macro.

6 Output

The program tells the computer to print the results of the memory copy to the screen using the `printf()` function. The computer reads the data from the given variables `Val1` and `Val2` and prints them to the screen as part of a message.

Preprocessor   Reserved words   Identifiers and symbols   Strings and numbers   Comments

Moving Memory

```
1    #include <stdio.h>
     #include <string.h>

2    main()
     {

3       int      Val1;
         int      Val2;

4       printf("Enter a numeric value : ");
        scanf("%d",&Val1);

5       memmove(&Val2, &Val1,sizeof(int));

6       printf("Value 1 is %d.  The moved value 2 is
           %d.\n", Val1, Val2);

     }
```

Moving memory is similar to copying memory in that it merely takes one block of memory and places it into another location. Again, C provides all the functionality necessary to perform this operation. One important thing to notice in this program is the similarity between copying and moving blocks of memory in C.

1 Include Statement

The #include statement tells the compiler that the named files should be included in the code. The include files provide prototypes for standard input and output, stdio.h, as well as some memory management functions, string.h.

2 Program Entry Point

The main() statement is the program's entry point and tells the C compiler where execution begins.

3 Declarations

The program tells the computer to allocate two integer variables. The variable named Val1 is used to store a value that you enter from the keyboard. The variable Val2 is used to store the moved value in Val1.

4 Data Entry

The program tells the computer to print the message Enter a numeric value : to the screen using the printf() function. The program waits for you to enter a number and to press Enter. The scanf() function stores the number you enter into the variable Val1.

Notice again the use of the ampersand operator in the `scanf()` function. This operator tells the computer to read the value entered at the keyboard and place it into the address where the integer variable `Val1` is located.

5 Copying Memory

The `memmove()` function (whose prototype is located in `string.h`) is called to move memory you specify. The variable `Val2` is passed to the function as the destination of the data to be moved. `Val1` is the origin and contains the number that was entered into the `scanf()` function.

Notice that each of the variables is preceded by an ampersand. This operator tells the function `memmove()` to use the addresses of the variables passed—just like in the `scanf()` function. The `memmove()` function moves the data out of the address of `Val1` and stores the data into the address of `Val2`. The first parameter of the function is always the destination of the move operation, whereas the second is always the source. The third parameter of the function tells how many bytes are to be moved from the address of `Val1` to the address of `Val2`. Recall that an `int` is only two bytes long so the third parameter is equal to 2—as retrieved with the `sizeof()` macro.

6 Output

The program tells the computer to print the results of the memory move to the screen using the `printf()` function. The computer reads the data from the given variables `Val1` and `Val2` and prints them to the screen as part of a message.

Copying Strings

```
#include <stdio.h>
#include <string.h>

main()
{
        char        String1[20];
        char        String2[20];

        printf("Enter a string : ");
        scanf("%s",String1);

        strcpy(String2, String1);
        printf("String 1 is %s.   String 2 is %s.\n",
          String1, String2);

        strncpy(String2, String1,2);
        String2[2] = '\0';
        printf("String 1 is %s.   String 2 is %s.\n",
            String1, String2);
}
```

1
2
3
4
5

Copying a string is similar to copying blocks of memory except that the functions for copying strings are specific to string operations only. You can use memory management functions on strings but not vice versa. The reason is that the string functions copy char data types up to and including the null terminator. Most regular blocks of memory have no null terminator, so the string function would not have any notion of where the block of memory ends.

1 Data Entry

The program tells the computer to print the message Enter a string : to the screen using the printf() function. The program waits for you to enter a string and to press Enter. The scanf() function stores the string you enter into the variable String1.

Recall the purpose of the ampersand operator? The ampersand tells the scanf() function to place the information entered at the keyboard into the address of the variable—a pointer. The reason that you do not use an ampersand here is that a pointer is already being passed to scanf() with the String1 variable.

2 Copying an Entire String

The strcpy() function is called to copy a string you specify. The variable String2 is passed to the function as the destination of the data to be copied. String1 is the origin and contains the string that was entered into the scanf() function. The function reads the block of memory for String1 and copies the string, up to and including the null terminator, over to String2.

The block of memory that the variable points to, in this instance, is 20 bytes long and contains the string that you entered. The strcpy() function copies the data out of the address of String1 and stores the data into the address of String2. The first parameter of the function is always the destination of the copy operation, whereas the second is always the source. There is no third size parameter, as with memcpy() or memmove(), because the function copies up to the null terminator of the source string.

3 Output

The program tells the computer to print the results of the string copy to the screen using the printf() function. The computer reads the data from the given variables String1 and String2 and prints them to the screen as part of a message.

4 Copying a Partial String

The strncpy() function is called to copy part of a string we specify. Use the variable String1 as the origin and String2 as the destination. The function reads the block of memory for String1 and copies the string, for the number of characters specified as the third parameter of the function call to String2.

The statement String2[2] = '\0'; places a null terminator at the end of the new string. Recall from Lessons 16 and 19 that the first element of an array is accessed at offset 0 which means that an offset of 2, as in this example, is actually the third element of String2. The placement of the null terminator with String2[2] = '\0'; terminates the two characters.

5 Initialization section

The program tells the computer to print the results of the partial string copy to the screen using the printf() function.

> **NOTE**
>
> String functions can cause your program to crash for no apparent reason. The most common reason for this is information you have handled in your program has either overwritten the end of the string or the string is not null terminated due to a partial copy or related operation.

Preprocessor   Reserved words   Identifiers and symbols   Strings and numbers   Comments

LESSON 45

Concatenating Strings

```c
#include <stdio.h>
#include <string.h>

main()
{
    char    String1[40];
    char    String2[20];
    int     length;

    printf("Enter the first string : ");
    scanf("%s",String1);
    printf("Enter the second string : ");
    scanf("%s",String2);

    length = strlen(String1);

    strcat(String1, String2);
    printf("The combined string is %s\n",String1);

    strncat(String1, String2,2);
    String1[length+2] = '\0';
    printf("The partial combined string is %s\n",
            String1, String2);
}
```

1 → `length = strlen(String1);`

2 → `strcat(String1, String2);`

3 → `printf("The combined string is %s\n",String1);`

4 → `strncat(String1, String2,2);` `String1[length+2] = '\0';`

5 → `printf("The partial combined string is %s\n", String1, String2);`

Occasionally, you have to bring two strings together into one. To do this, you have to take one string and copy it to the end of another string, always making sure that you have enough room in the destination string to hold both strings.

1 Length of a String

You have to determine the length of the original string for the program to know how to manage it when you perform a partial concatenation. The null terminator is overwritten and you have to know exactly where to place the terminator in the newly created string.

2 Concatenating Entire Strings

The `strcat()` function is called to concatenate the strings that are passed to it as parameters. The variable `String1` is passed to the function as the destination of the original string. `String2` is the origin of the string concatenated to `String1`. The function reads the block of memory for `String2` and concatenates the string, up to and including the null terminator, over to `String1`, placing it at the end of the string.

3 Output

The program prints the results of the concatenation on-screen with `printf()`.

4 Concatenating Partial Strings

The `strncat()` function is called to concatenate part of one string onto another full string. Again, use the variable `String2` as the origin and `String1` as the destination. The third parameter of the function, a value of 2, tells the function to concatenate the first two characters of `String2` to the end of `String1`.

Remember that `strcat()` concatenates an entire string, including the null terminator located at the end of the string. In this program, the partial concatenation of 2 characters from `String2` onto `String1` causes the null terminator of `String1` to be overwritten. The statement `String1[length+2] = '\0';` places a null terminator at the end of the new string. The index `length+2` tells the computer where to place the null terminator—`'\0'`. The `length` variable contains the length of `String1` while the addition of the 2 takes into account the 2 characters that were concatenated from `String2`.

5 More Output

The program tells the computer to print the results of the partial string copy to the screen using the `printf()` function.

NOTE

When you take the length of a string using `strlen()`, you are determining the number of characters in the string up to but not including the null terminator. The actual null terminator is located at one position past the length of the string—`length + 1`.

WHY WORRY?

Make sure that the destination string is large enough to handle the original string and the string to be added during the concatenation operation. If this is not the case, you might overwrite important data in memory.

Preprocessor   Reserved words   Identifiers and symbols   Strings and numbers   Comments

Looking at String Sizes

```
#include <stdio.h>
#include <string.h>

main()
{
        char    String[40];
1       int     length;
        int     size;

2       printf("Enter a string : ");
        scanf("%s",String);

3       length = strlen(String);
4       size = sizeof(String);

5       printf("The size of '%s' is %d and the
            length is %d\n",
                String,size,length);

}
```

Whenever you are dealing with strings, you are handling a data type that has two different measurements: its size and its length. So what's the difference? You have seen what the size of a data type is by using the sizeof() macro. This size tells you how big the block of memory is that is marked for a string variable. The length is the actual number of characters stored in the variable that make up a usable string. This length is from the first character up to the null terminator.

1 Declarations

The computer allocates memory for two ints and one string. The string variable String is used to store the information that you enter at the keyboard. The length and size variables are used to store the length of the string in the variable and the size of the memory allocated for the variable respectively.

2 Data Entry

The printf() prints the message Enter a string : to the screen, asking you to enter a string at the keyboard. The program waits for you to enter the string and to press Enter. The `scanf()` function stores the string you enter into the variable `String`.

3 Length of a String

The length of the string stored in the variable `String` is taken by passing `String` to the function `strlen()`. The function looks at the string and determines the number of characters up to, but not including, the null terminator for the string. The number of characters determined to be in the string by the function is returned and stored in the variable `length`.

4 Size of a String

The size of the variable `String` is taken by passing the variable to the macro `sizeof()`. The macro looks at the string and determines the number of bytes allocated for the string variable. The number of bytes that the macro determines are available for the variable is returned and stored in the variable `size`.

5 Output

The program reads the three variables from memory and uses the `printf()` function to output the results.

The one thing to notice is that the value of the `size` variable and the value of the `length` variable are quite different. The value stored in the `size` variable is the actual number of bytes allocated for the `String`. In this program, `size` equals 40 because the variable `String` was declared to have 40 characters. The `length` variable stores the value equal to the number of characters preceding the null terminator and is dependent on what is entered for the `scanf()` function to store in `String`. For example, if you enter the word *Moose* when the program asks for input, the `length` returned would be 5, but the `size` remains 40.

LESSON 47

Converting Strings and Integers

```c
#include <stdio.h>
#include <stdlib.h>

main()
{
    char    Age[5];
    int     age;

    printf("Enter your age : ");
    scanf("%s",Age);

    age = atoi(Age);
    printf("Your integer age is %d.\n",age);

    itoa(age,Age,16);
    printf("Your string hex age is %s.\n",Age);
}
```

1

2

3

4

In a data entry screen for a database management system, your users can enter information in the form of strings. There are times, however, when these strings have to be converted for storage in the actual database file. Information such as age and monthly income could be entered as strings and converted to integers for storage. The conversion from strings to integers is important for operations that involve numeric calculations on the values. You cannot add strings together to provide a numeric sum. Instead these strings must be converted to numbers for the calculation. But

then, when you want to read the information back out for display, you have to convert the integers from the file back to strings for the entry screen. In C, the capability to perform such conversions is as simple as a function call.

1 Declarations

The program tells the computer to allocate two variables. The first variable, Age, is given a block of memory five bytes long of type char. This variable is used to store the age you enter from the keyboard. The second variable, age, is of type int and is used to store the converted integer variable from the string. Notice that the two variables `age` and `Age` are the same word, but C treats them differently. Because C is case-sensitive, `Age` looks different to C than does age.

2 Data Entry

The `printf()` function prints the message `Enter your age :` to the screen, asking you to enter your age at the keyboard. The program waits for you to enter the value and to press Enter. The `scanf()` function stores the age you enter into the variable `Age`.

3 String to Integer Conversion

The function `atoi()` is called with the string `Age` passed as the single parameter to the function. The function reads the information stored in the variable and converts it to an `int`. The converted value is then returned to the variable `age` for storage. If you enter anything other than a number, the function converts the information to a value of 0.

The program then reads the converted value from `age` and prints it to the screen with a message using the `printf()` function.

4 Integer to String Conversion

The function `itoa()` is called with three parameters. The first parameter is the `int` variable `age` that you want to convert into a string. The second variable `Age` is the string in which you place the converted integer. The final parameter is the base for the conversion. In this program, you tell the computer to convert the integer to a string using base 16, hexadecimal. You can also tell the computer to convert the integer using base 10, binary, or even base 8 octal.

For all practical purposes, hexadecimal, octal, binary, and decimal all provide the same numeric output from a program. The output format is dependant on your particular application, however, hexadecimal and binary provide you with an output that details the specifics of numeric values and are used mostly for program debugging purposes. With hexadecimal and binary you can see the specific details of the numeric values—the states of the individual bits that make up the bytes. Octal is rarely used except in older systems.

The program then reads the converted value from `Age` and prints it to the screen, in hexadecimal, with a message using the `printf()` function.

Converting Strings and Floats

```c
#include <stdio.h>
#include <stdlib.h>

main()
{
    char      AmountDue[20];
    double    amountdue;

    printf("Enter the amount due : ");
    scanf("%s",AmountDue);

    amountdue = atof(AmountDue);
    printf("The amount due is '%s' -> %g\n",
           AmountDue, amountdue);
}
```

1
2
3
4
5

Now that you know how to convert integers to strings, look at converting floating point decimals. The reason for using such a conversion follows in line with our database management example for the integers. For example, you might have your users enter a decimal for the amount due on a given bill. The users enter it as a string, and the program converts the string to a float for storage in, say, your company's billing database. Now that the string is converted to a numeric value, a float, the billing system can use these values to calculate totals for a given bill. Remember from Lesson 47 that you cannot add strings; they must be converted to some type of numeric data type before any calculations can be performed on them.

1 Include Statement

The #include statement tells the compiler that the named files should be included in the code.

2 Program Entry Point

The main() statement is the program's entry point, and it tells the C compiler where execution begins.

3 Declarations

The program tells the computer to allocate two variables. The first variable, AmountDue, is given a block of memory 20 bytes long of type char. This variable is used to store a decimal value that you enter from the keyboard. The second variable, amountdue, is of type double and is used to store the converted floating point decimal from the string.

Notice here that the two variables `amountdue` and `AmountDue` are the same word, but C treats them differently because they have different cases. Because C is case-sensitive, `AmountDue` looks different to C than does `amountdue`.

4 Data Entry

The `printf()` function prints the message `Enter the amount due :` to the screen, asking you to enter a decimal value at the keyboard. The program waits for you to enter the value and to press Enter. The `scanf()` function stores the string you enter into the variable `AmountDue`.

5 String to Floating Point Conversion

The function `atof()` is called with the string `AmountDue` passed as the single parameter to the function. The function reads the information stored in the variable and converts it to a `double`. The converted value is returned to the variable `amountdue` for storage. If you enter anything other than a number, the function converts the information to a value of 0.

The program then reads the converted value from `amountdue` as well as the string stored in `AmountDue` and prints it to the screen with a message using the `printf()` function.

LESSON 49
Array Indexing

```c
#include <stdio.h>

main()
{
    int     IntegerArray[5];
    int     loopcount;

    IntegerArray[0] = 10;
    IntegerArray[1] = 20;
    IntegerArray[2] = 30;
    IntegerArray[3] = 40;
    IntegerArray[4] = 50;

    for(loopcount = 0; loopcount < 5; loopcount ++)
        printf("Offset #%d is at %d with a value of %d\n",
            loopcount,&IntegerArray[loopcount],
            IntegerArray[loopcount]);
}
```

Arrays, as you know, are collections of a particular data type. You can have an array of ints, an array of chars, and even an array of arrays. One of the many reasons for using an array is to reduce the number of variables used in a program. Let's say that you have to keep track of 1,000 numbers for some reason. An easy way is to create 1,000 individual variables. Not only would you have to come up with 1,000 unique names, but your program would become almost unintelligible due to the decisions that would have to be made as to which of the variables to use for a given situation. Arrays solve this problem easily!

1 Include Statement

The #include statement tells the compiler that the named files should be included in the code.

2 Program Entry Point

The main() statement is the program's entry point and it tells the C compiler where execution begins.

3 Declarations

The first variable declared, IntegerArray, is given a block of memory equal to five ints. This turns out to be 10 bytes long. The second variable, `loopcount`, is an `int` and is used to control a loop for display of the values in `IntegerArray`.

4 Initialization

The program accesses each of the integers in the arrays and sets them to a particular value. The first element of the array is accessed by going to offset 0 of the array—`IntegerArray[0] = 10;`. In a simplistic view, the computer takes the value of the index and multiplies it by the size of the elements in the array to access a given element.

To access element 3, you provide the index of 2. The computer takes the size of an integer, 2, and multiplies it by the given index of 2. The computer then knows that it must go past the fourth byte of the array to reach element 3 of that array—`IntegerArray[2] = 30;`. After the element is accessed, the computer either retrieves or sets the block of memory marked for that element based on the commands you provided in your program.

5 Output

A loop, using the `loopcount` variable, is used to access each element of the array. The computer starts with `loopcount` equal to 0. It then goes to the offset in the array specified by `loopcount` and prints the value of `loopcount`, the address of that element of the array, and the value of `IntegerArray` at the given offset. The loop continues, incrementing `loopcount` at each pass, until the value of `loopcount` equals 5.

One thing to pay attention to when you run this program is the address being printed by the `printf()` statement. The first address printed, offset 0, is the beginning address of the array. Each subsequent address printed is 2 higher than the previous. This corresponds to the fact that the array of type `int` has contiguous elements in memory, each two bytes long.

WHAT DOES IT MEAN?

The *offset* is the number of elements that you have to go through within an array to reach an element within the array The *index* is a value provided to access a given element of an array. Put simply, you provide an index to access an element at a particular offset within an array.

LESSON 50

Structure Access

```c
#include <stdio.h>

struct      NameStruct
{
    char        Name[20];
    char        Address[40];
    int         Age;
};

main()
{
    struct NameStruct       Record;

    printf("Enter your name : ");
    scanf("%s",Record.Name);

    printf("Enter your city  : ");
    scanf("%s",Record.Address);

    printf("Enter your age : ");
    scanf("%d",&Record.Age);

    printf("Hello %d year old %s in %s\n",
        Record.Age, Record.Name, Record.Address);
}
```

1
2
3
4
5

Structures enable you to encapsulate several different data types into one larger data type. One of the more common uses for a structure is the creation and management of database records. Each member of the structure coincides with a field in a record. Accessing each of these members is as simple as accessing a regular variable.

1 Structure Definition

The program defines the structure it is going to use throughout the program. This one definition can be used as though it were a standard C data type. The structure, NameStruct, contains three members. Two of the members are strings, Name being 20 characters and `Address` being 40 characters. The third member is an `int` data type called `Age`.

2 Program Entry Point

The `main()` statement is the program's entry point and it tells the C compiler where execution begins.

3 Declarations

Before you can use a structure, it has to be declared as a variable. As you can see, the keyword `struct` precedes the name of the structure `NameStruct`. The last word in the statement is the variable `Record` that is to be used to access the elements of the structure. This tells the computer to assign the characteristics of the structure `NameStruct` to a block of memory marked by `Record`.

Because the structure definition can be treated like a standard C data type, you can declare as many variables of that data type as required in your program. You can even declare an array of `NameStructs` if required and access each instance of that structure by providing an index to that structure in the array.

4 Data Entry

The computer prompts you for the entry of three pieces of information to fill up the variable `Record`. The program, using the `printf()` statement, asks you to enter your name, city, and age. The `scanf()` function stores each entry that you make into the respective members of the variable `Record`.

Notice how the members of the variable are accessed. You access members by using the dot operator separating the variable name and the member name. To access the name member you use `Record.Name`, address is `Record.Address`, and age is `Record.Age`. The computer uses the member names of `NameStruct` to access the data internal to the variable `Record`.

5 Output

The program uses the `printf()` function to print the contents of the variable `Record`. Again, use the dot operator to extract the values of the members of `Record`. The computer accesses each of these members as though they were standard variables and displays them to the screen as part of a message.

LESSON 51

Typecasting

```
1 ──► #include <stdio.h>

2 ──► main()
     {
3 ──► int      IntegerVar;
  ──► char     CharVar;
  ──► float    FloatVar;

4 ──► printf("Enter a number : ");
  ──► scanf("%f",&FloatVar);

5 ──► CharVar = (char)FloatVar;
  ──► IntegerVar = (int)FloatVar;

6 ──► printf("FLOAT : %g        INT : %d        CHAR : %c\n",
        FloatVar, IntegerVar,CharVar);
     }
```

To follow the ideas of converting information from one type to another, let's take a look at typecasting. Typecasting helps you to take one data type and convert it to another. This is unlike the string to numeric conversion that was discussed previously. This type of conversion allows you to take an `int` and convert it to a `float` or take a char and convert it to an `int`. Such type conversion provides you with the flexibility to take a type and make it another without any function call. Everything is handled at the assignment level of the C language.

1 Include Statement

The `#include` statement tells the compiler that the named files should be included in the code.

2 Program Entry Point

The `main()` statement is the program's entry point and it tells the C compiler where execution begins.

3 Declarations

The program declares three variables. Each of these variables is allocated by the computer to use in the typecasting operation. `IntegerVar` is a two-byte `int` variable, `CharVariable` is a one-byte `char`, and `FloatVar` is a two-byte `float`.

4 Data Entry

The program tells the computer to print the message `Enter a number :` to the screen. The computer waits with the `scanf()` function until you enter a floating point value with the keyboard. When you enter a number at the keyboard and press Enter, the `scanf()` function reads the value and stores it into the variable `FloatVar`.

5 Typecasting

The program first reads the values from the four-byte `float` and converts them to a one-byte `char` using the statement `CharVar = (char)FloatVar`. The program then reads the `float` variable `FloatVar` and converts it to an `int`. The resulting conversion is stored in the variable `IntegerVar` using `IntegerVar = (int)FloatVar`. For both typecasting statements, the variable that is to be converted is preceded by the data type into which the variable is converted. To convert to a `char`, the `float` is preceded by `(char)`, whereas the conversion to an `int` is preceded by `(int)`. The data types enclosed in the parentheses are the data types into which the value in `FloatVar` is converted. The variables to the left of the assignment operator (`=`) are where the converted value from `FloatVar` is stored.

During the typecast conversion, the computer reads the value from the variable `FloatVar`. It takes the value and, through the typecast operator `(char)`, converts the floating point value into a character. This operator tells the computer that it should take the `float`, convert it to a `char`, and store it into `CharVar`. The same type of operation occurs with `IntegerVar`.

The difference between the `float` and the `char` is that the `float` has a much larger range than the `char`. If the value in `FloatVar` exceeds the maximum value of `CharVar`, the casted values will lose significance. The same applies to the `int` variable `IntegerVar`.

6 Output

The program uses the `printf()` function to print the contents of the variables `IntegerVar`, `CharVar`, and `FloatVar`. The computer goes to the memory marked for each variable, extracts the values, and prints them as part of a message.

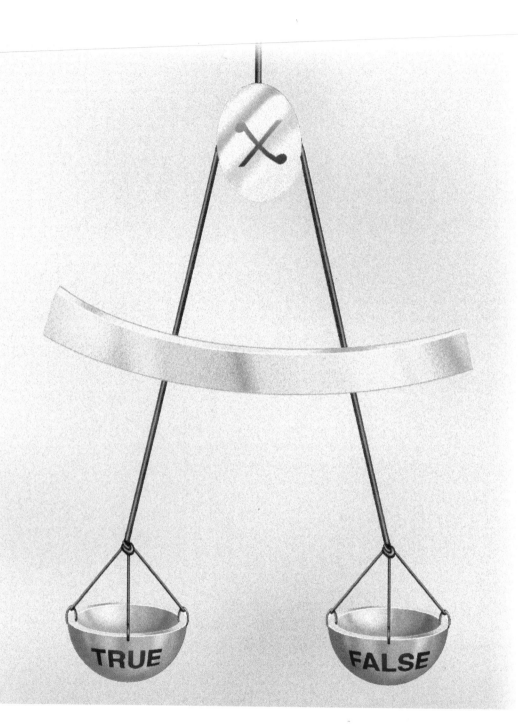

PART 9

Decisions and Repetition

Making decisions and performing operations based on those decisions is one of the many powerful functions of a computer. A computer can analyze information and, based on criteria that you provide, make a quick decision as to how to handle a particular operation. If the idea of computers making decisions based on data seems a little strange, think about how you make decisions. For example, suppose you're expecting an important letter. You go out to your mailbox and look inside. If there is mail in the box you remove it; otherwise, you complain about the postal system. In either case, you have made a decision based on whether there is mail in the mailbox.

Program flow is the order in which a program executes its code. Your programs so far in this book have had sequential program flow, starting at the first line of the program and working down to the last line. Truth is, almost all program code executes sequentially. However, virtually every program reaches a point where a decision must be made about a piece of data. The program must then analyze the data, decide what to do about it, and jump to the appropriate section of code. This decision-making process is a very important part of a computer and all programs that run on it. Virtually no useful programs can be written without some form of decision-making operation.

When a program breaks the sequential flow and jumps, or branches, to a new section of code, it is called *branching*. When this branching is based on a decision, the program is performing *conditional branching*. When no decision-making is involved and the program always branches when it encounters a branching instruction, the program is performing *unconditional branching*. Unconditional branching is basically a redundant programming method—the program will perform an action regardless of a situation. The important branching methods are those that actually change the course of the program's flow.

Most conditional branching occurs when the program executes an `if` statement. The `if` statement compares data and decides what to do next based on the result of the comparison. For example, you have probably seen programs that print menus on-screen. To select a menu item, you often type its selection number. When the program receives your input, it checks the number you entered and decides what to do. The entire decision for the `if` is based on a true or false return on the comparison. If the result of the comparison is true, an action is taken; otherwise, the action is skipped and regular program execution resumes.

Looping Constructs

Each type of looping construct works best in different circumstances. For example, a `for` loop should be used only for loops that always execute from the starting limit to the ending limit. If you find yourself trying to get out of a `for` loop before the loop has run its course, you should probably be using a `while` loop or `do-while` loop.

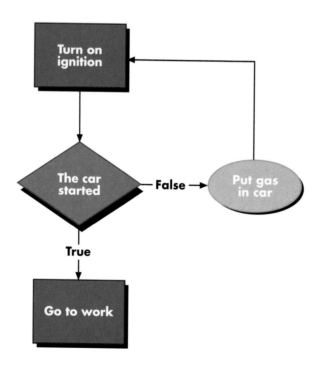

The `else` statement provides a default outcome for an `if` statement. The `else` is the action taken if the result of the `if` is false. A default outcome doesn't help much, however, in an `if` statement that has to deal with more than two possible outcomes.

So, what if you have more than two possible outcomes to a given situation? Because the `if` statement can only handle two possibilities based on the outcome of a decision, what do you do? The `switch-case` statement can solve that problem! A `switch-case` statement can cover dozens of possible outcomes for a given decision. You can program the `switch-case` to execute one of many different possible actions based on all of the results of a given decision. Taking the menu example again, the computer can simply determine which selection was made and immediately go to the operation that should occur based on that selection.

Looping is another form of decision-making and uses comparisons and decisions quite extensively. Probably the most often used loop in C is the `for` loop, which instructs a program to perform a block of code a specified number of times. You could, for example, use a `for` loop to instruct your computer to print 10,000 address labels. Since you don't currently have an address file, say you want to print your name on the screen six times. The `for` loop would simply print your name, decide if it has been printed six times, and if so, exit. Otherwise, it would print it again and check.

Another type of loop you can use in your programs is the `while` loop. Unlike a `for` loop, which loops the number of times given in the loop limits, a `while` loop continues running until its control expression becomes true. The *control expression* is a Boolean expression much like the Boolean expressions used with `if` statements. In other words, any expression that evaluates to true or false can be used as a control expression for a `while` loop.

WHAT DOES IT MEAN?

Boolean expressions allow you to determine if a set of conditions is true or false. For instance, the Boolean expression 9 > 10 AND 8 > 6 is false since 9 is not greater than 10. In this type of an expression, the comparisons on either side of the AND must be true for the entire Boolean expression to be true.

A relative of the `while` loop is the `do-while` loop. This loop operates in the same manner as the `while` except that the loop decision mechanism is at the bottom of the loop rather than at the top. This mechanism enables the loop to run at least one time and evaluate the comparison values immediately after the code executes.

Now take a look at looping and decision-making in C. The one important thing to remember throughout the following lessons is that you have seen this all before in previous lessons. The only difference between what you have seen and what you will see here is that you are merely taking a different angle on the uses of C's functions and capabilities.

LESSON 52

DO-WHILE Loops

```c
#include <stdio.h>

main()
{
    int      IntegerVar;

    do
    {
        printf("Enter a number : ");
        scanf("%d",&IntegerVar);
        printf("\nYou entered : %d\n",IntegerVar);
    }while(IntegerVar > 5);

    printf("Correct Guess : %d\n",IntegerVar);
}
```

1
2
3
4
5

Repetitive operations are important for many tasks in computers—everything from assembly line automation to complex calculations to simple data entry. The one thing that a do-while loop brings to the table is a level of intelligence. The loop repeats its block of code only as long as a given condition exists. The two forms of a do-while loop are the do-while and the while. The while evaluates expressions at the top of the loop and the do-while evaluates expressions at the bottom.

1 Declarations

The program declares only one int variable. The computer allocates a two-byte block of memory for the variable that will be used to store values that you enter from the keyboard.

2 Start of the DO Loop

The do statement tells the computer that the code that follows is the beginning of a do loop. All code following the do statement and preceding the while()—the code between the curly brackets—is executed repetitively until a condition exists that ends the loop.

3 Internals of the Loop

The program tells the computer to print a message to the screen using the `printf()` function. The message requests that you enter a number. The `scanf()` function waits until you enter a number and press Enter, then stores the value you entered into the `IntegerVar` variable. The program then tells the computer to print another message to the screen containing the value that you entered.

4 Loop Condition

The program uses the value that you enter to determine if the program should execute the code of the loop again or exit. The condition reads `while(IntegerVar > 5)` which tells the computer to perform the loop as long as the value that you enter is greater than 5.

As long as you enter anything greater than 5, the code inside of the do-while will execute. If you enter a value that is less than 5, the loop exits and the program continues.

In a `while` loop, this statement is located where the `do` is located. The reason for the two different methods of using conditional looping has to do with where you want to evaluate the condition. In some circumstances, you have to evaluate at the top of the loop, and in others you might want the code within the loop to execute once, so evaluate it at the bottom. The `while()` statement is used the same way in either case; it is just located in a different part of the loop.

5 Output

After the loop exits, the program tells the computer to print a message `Correct Guess :` with the last value you entered. The last value entered is less than 5 to cause the loop to exit.

WHY WORRY?

Control expressions in `while` and `do-while` loops can become so complex that they may not end up with the result you require. Keep loop-control expressions simple, and be sure they provide the logic you want.

LESSON 53

FOR Loops

```c
#include <stdio.h>

main()
{
    int     IntegerVar;

    for(IntegerVar = 0; IntegerVar < 5; IntegerVar ++)
    {
        printf("\nThe computer entered : %d\n",
            IntegerVar);
    }

    printf("Final value : %d\n", IntegerVar);
}
```

1

2

3

The for loop provides a way to perform repetitive operations much like the while and do-while loops. Rather than basing its condition on the state of a variable inside of the loop, the for loop executes the loop code a set number of times. To manage the loop, a counter exists that counts up or down until it reaches a value that causes the loop to exit.

1 Declarations

The program declares only one int variable. This variable, IntegerVar, is used by the program to keep track of the loop count within the for loop.

2 The FOR Loop

The `for(IntegerVar = 0; IntegerVar < 5; IntegerVar ++)` statement tells the computer to first set the `IntegerVar` variable equal to the value 0. The value that the loop variable is set to can be any starting value that you require for the program. In most circumstances, you can use the value generated by the loop count variable to provide indices for sequential access to the elements of an array.

The second parameter, following the semicolon, tells the computer that the code within the loop continues as long as the value stored in `IntegerVar` is less than 5. You may use any logical expression here to provide the loop with a condition to tell the loop when it is to exit.

The third parameter is the increment statement for the loop. After each pass through the loop, the computer compares the value in `IntegerVar` to 5 and, if it is less than 5, it increments the value in `IntegerVar`. This increment statement was covered in more detail in Part 6 on mathematics.

Each pass through the loop, the program tells the computer to print a message using the `printf()` statement. The message prints to the screen and tells the current loop count for the variable `IntegerVar`.

3 Output

After the variable `IntegerVar` reaches the limit set by the `for` statement, the loop exits. The program tells the computer to print a message `Final Value :` with the last value incremented by the `for` loop. The last value that the variable `IntegerVar` reached is 5 because that exceeds the condition set by the second parameter of the `for` statement.

WHY WORRY?

If the control variable is not incremented correctly, a loop can carry on forever. This condition is known as an *infinite loop*, and it can cause programmers mental problems. If a program does not increment the control variable and test it correctly, the program may end up executing the loop forever rather than just the desired number of times.

LESSON 54

IF

```c
#include <stdio.h>

main()
{
    int     IntegerVar;

    printf("Enter a number : ");
    scanf("%d",&IntegerVar);
    if(IntegerVar > 5 && IntegerVar < 10)
    {
        printf("%d is  greater than 5 and less than
            10\n", IntegerVar);
    }
}
```

The `if` statement is one of the more frequently used decision-making mechanisms in C. The `if` statement provides you with incredible flexibility in making quick decisions on whether to execute a block of code.

1 Declarations

The program declares only one `int` variable. This variable is to store a value that you enter at the keyboard.

2 Data Entry

The computer prints the message Enter a number : on the screen. The `scanf()` function waits until you enter the number and press

Enter. After the number is entered, the value is stored into the block of memory marked for `IntegerVar`.

3 The IF Decision

A simple `if` statement includes the keyword `if` followed by a *Boolean expression*—an expression that evaluates to either true or false. These expressions are surrounded by parentheses. Follow the parentheses with the statement that you want executed if the Boolean expression is true.

The statement `if(IntegerVar > 5 && IntegerVar < 10)` compares the value you entered to two numbers. The computer first compares `IntegerVar` to the value of `5`, and if the value in `IntegerVar` is greater than 5, the comparison continues.

The `&&` operator is the Boolean AND operator and tells the computer that both conditions must be true for the `if` statement to execute its code. If the first comparison of `IntegerVar > 5` is false, the entire `if` statement is false and no more comparisons are executed. This is called *short circuit* Boolean evaluation. If a Boolean evaluation turns up false before its evaluation is complete, the computer aborts the rest of the evaluation instead of wasting time evaluating something that will be false anyway.

The final comparison looks at `IntegerVar` to make sure that it is less than 10. If it is, the `if` statement's condition is true. Again, the only way that the final comparison will occur is if the first comparison is true.

4 Output

If the condition of the `if` statement is true, meaning that you did enter a value between 5 and 10, the program prints a message containing the value that you entered. If you enter a value on either side of the boundaries of 5 and 10, the `printf()` function is skipped and program execution continues.

WHAT DOES IT MEAN?

Short circuit Boolean evaluation is a method of comparing logical expressions up to the point that the expression is no longer true. For example, 1 > 2 AND 9 < 10 is a logical expression. For an AND expression to be true, both sides must be true. As you can see, 1 > 2 is definitely false, so the computer short circuits the evaluation and does not evaluate 9 < 10 even though it is true.

LESSON 55

IF-ELSE

```
1  → #include <stdio.h>

2  → main()
      {
3         → int      IntegerVar;

4         → printf("Enter a number : ");
          → scanf("%d",&IntegerVar);

5         → if(IntegerVar > 5 && IntegerVar < 10)
            {
6               → printf("%d is  greater than 5 and less than
                → 10\n", IntegerVar);
            }
          → else
          → {
7               → printf("%d is  not greater than 5 and less
                → than 10\n", IntegerVar);
          }
      → }
```

The one problem with the previous program is that if the `if` statement is false, there is no output at all—nothing to tell you that the value entered was greater than 10 or less than 5. There is a solution to that problem with the `if-else` combination. The `if-else` statement gives you a chance to execute a block of code regardless of whether `if` evaluates to true or false.

1 Include Statement

The `#include` statement tells the compiler that the named files should be included into the code.

2 Program Entry Point

The `main()` statement is the program's entry point and it tells the C compiler where execution begins.

3 Declarations

The program declares only one `int` variable. This variable is used to store a value that you enter at the keyboard.

4 Data Entry

The computer prints the message `Enter a number :` on the screen. The `scanf()` function waits until you enter the number and press Enter. After the number is entered, the value is stored into the block of memory marked for `IntegerVar`.

5 The IF Decision

The statement `if(IntegerVar > 5 && IntegerVar < 10)` compares the value you entered to two numbers. The computer first compares `IntegerVar` to the value of 5, and if the value in `IntegerVar` is greater than 5, the comparison continues.

The `&&` operator is the Boolean AND operator and tells the computer that both conditions must be true for the `if` statement to execute its code.

The final comparison looks at `IntegerVar` to make sure that it is less than 10. If it is, the `if` statement's condition is true. Again, the only way the final comparison will occur is if the first comparison is true.

6 Output

If the condition of the `if` statement is true, meaning that you did enter a value between 5 and 10, the program prints a message containing the value that you entered. If you enter a value on either side of the boundaries of 5 and 10, this `printf()` function is skipped.

7 ELSE Condition

If the condition in the `if` statement is false, meaning that you entered a value less than 5 or greater than 10, the program skips to the `else` statement. The `printf()` executes, printing a message telling you that the number you entered was not within the boundaries specified.

The `else` statement gives you a method of capturing two possible conditions of an evaluation as opposed to one with a simple `if`. In most circumstances, you want to provide an `else` to execute a block of code if the evaluation of the `if` turns out to be false.

Preprocessor Reserved words Identifiers and symbols Strings and numbers Comments

LESSON 56

SWITCH-CASE

```c
#include <stdio.h>

main()
{
    int      IntegerVar;

    printf("Enter a numeric selection : ");
    scanf("%d",&IntegerVar);

    switch(IntegerVar)
    {
        case  0 :
                printf("You selected 0\n");
                break;
        case 1 :
                printf("You selected 1\n");
                break;
        default :
                printf("Your selection was invalid\n");
                break;
    }
    printf("The End\n");
}
```

1

2

3

4

5

6

The `switch-case` statement enables you to make multiple decisions and execute one of dozens of blocks of code based on a result of one of the decisions. There is no true or false evaluation involved in the execution of a `switch-case` statement; however, the computer must match a certain pattern in a list of possibilities before a block of code is executed.

1 Declarations

The program declares only one `int` variable. This variable is used to store a value that you enter at the keyboard.

2 Data Entry

The computer prints the message `Enter a numeric selection :` on the screen. The `scanf()` function waits until you enter the number and press Enter. After the number is

entered, the value is stored into the block of memory marked for
IntegerVar.

3 The SWITCH Statement

The switch statement takes an ordinal value and determines which block
of code to execute. The value, an int or a char, provides a numeric value
that is located in a list of possible statements immediately following the
statement.

4 The CASE Statement

The case statement provides a marker for the switch statement. This
marker represents a block of code that is executed if the switch statement
receives that value. In this program, case 0 : represents a block of code
executed if the switch receives a value of 0 from IntegerVar.

5 Code Execution

If a 0 is entered in the scanf() function, this block of code will execute.
The program tells the computer to print the message You selected 0 to
the screen. The break statement tells the computer that execution of this
block of code ends here. After the computer sees the break, it skips to the
end of the entire switch-case statement and continues program
execution.

If you forget to place a break at the end of a block of code, the computer
will continue into the next block of code and print You selected 1 also.

6 The DEFAULT Case

The default case for a switch-case is similar to the else of an if-else.
The default is the block of code that executes if the switch obtains a
value not represented by any case. In this program, if you enter any value
other than 0 or 1, the default will be called. The default code in this
program prints the message Your selection was invalid telling you of
your entry error.

WHY WORRY?

If you forget to place a
break at the end of a
block of code for a given
case statement, the
computer will execute
straight through until it
either comes to the end
of the switch-case or it
does find a break.

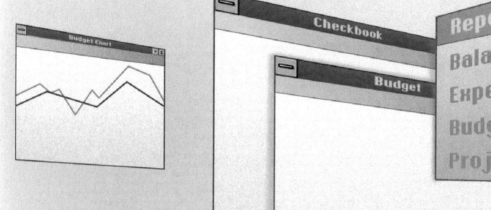

PART 10

Screen Input/Output

A computer wouldn't be much of a machine if you didn't have a way of getting data in and out of it in a usable form. For example, say you want to type a letter to one of your friends. Your first task is to get the characters that make up the letter into your computer's memory where you can manipulate them. You must use one of the computer's input devices—in this case, the keyboard—to type your letter, placing it into memory one character at a time.

So, how do you know what you are typing? You can enter the characters for the letter, but how can you tell what you have typed into the computer? Most personal computers come with video capabilities that enable you to see what you are entering at the keyboard. As the information is entered, it is displayed on the screen in the format of the letter that you are typing. The video display is merely a replica of the information stored in your computer's memory.

The processes of moving data in and out of a computer are called, appropriately enough, *input* and *output* (or I/O, for short). There are many kinds of input and output, but you have to know only a couple to get started with the C programming language. In this chapter, you learn to retrieve data from a user and print that data on your computer's screen.

WHAT DOES IT MEAN?

Input devices, such as a keyboard or a mouse, transfer data from you to your computer. *Output devices*, such as printers and monitors, transfer data from the computer back to you. Some devices, such as disk drives, are both input and output devices.

Most input and output is controlled by the program that is currently running in your computer's memory. If you load a program that doesn't use the keyboard, no matter how much you type, the program will not notice your keystrokes. Likewise, if a program wasn't designed to use your screen, you have no way of accessing the screen when running that program. Obviously, then, if it's up to a program to control your computer's input and output,

every programming language must contain commands for input and output. In fact, a programming language without I/O commands is about as useful to you as a book of matches is to a fish. By providing commands for putting data into the computer and getting data back out again, a computer language enables you to create interactive programs.

WHAT DOES IT MEAN?

Interactive programs enable the user and the computer to communicate with each other. For example, the computer can output a question to the user by printing the question on the screen. The user can then answer the question using the keyboard.

Receiving input from the keyboard occurs in several different ways. You can read `chars`, `ints`, `floats`, `doubles`, strings, and other C and user-defined data types right from the keyboard. One of the functions, called `gets()`, retrieves a string from the keyboard and stores it into a string variable that you declared in your program. Another function, in line with `gets()`, is `getchar()`. In actuality, `getchar()` is a macro that extracts information, one character at a time, from the keyboard and stores it into a `char` or `int` data type. A final function, called `scanf()`, enables formatted input from the keyboard. The `gets()` and `getchar()` functions only accept character data types while `scanf()` accepts all of the different data types of C and places the input information into the specified variables. A variation of `scanf()` is `sscanf()`; `sscanf` works in conjunction with `gets()`. The function `sscanf()` reads formatted input from a string and not directly from the keyboard.

WHAT DOES IT MEAN?

Formatted input involves the retrieval of information in a particular format. For example, in one input statement you can retrieve a string, a `char`, and an `int`. Each of these data types is formatted specifically for the variables for which they are used in the function.

Output is a very straightforward process in C. Simply pass the variables you want to output to the screen to a function, and C takes care of the rest. Very simple, very straightforward. For starters, you have a `putchar()` function and a `puts()` function that output a character and a string to the screen respectively. You pass a string to `puts()` and the entire string is written to the screen, for example, a data entry screen for a database management application. These

are similar to the input functions for strings and `chars`, except that they go in the opposite direction. The final output function is `printf()`. This function is used numerous times in the sample programs of this book. In this part, however, the many different uses of `printf()` are demonstrated.

Input and output are two very important topics of computer programming. If the computer has no input, then what is it to do? Then if it has no output, how are you to know what is going on? There are many different methods that a computer uses to receive input and output information, but for this part you stick to standard keyboard and screen I/O. Pay close attention to this section because not only does it divulge some topics discussed earlier, it also gives you a view of the complete cycle of a program—Input to Process to Output.

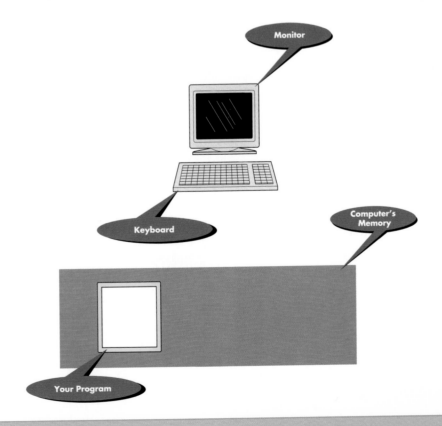

LESSON 57
Outputting Strings

```
1    #include <stdio.h>

2    main()
     {
3        /*Declare two variables*/
         char     String[30];
         int      RetVal;

4        /*Request user input for the String*/
         printf("Enter your name : ");
         scanf("%s",String);

5        /*Print a format string to the screen along
            with the entered selection*/
         printf("Your name is  :   ");
         RetVal = puts(String);

6        /*Print the value returned by puts() to the
            screen*/
7        printf("\nReturned Value is '%d'\n", RetVal);
     }
```

Handling the output of strings is similar to handling their processing. There are functions that handle string output to the screen that understand the concept of null-terminated strings. The function puts() takes a string variable, with the null terminator, and writes it to the screen. Uses for this function vary between applications, but its most common use is for the display of information in database management systems' entry screens.

1 Include Statement

The #include statement tells the compiler that the named files should be included into the code.

2 Program Entry Point

The main() statement is the program's entry point and tells the C compiler where execution begins.

3 Declarations

To use the `puts()` function, you must declare at least one string variable. In this lesson, the program declares a variable named `String` dimensioned to 30 `char`s. The program also declares an `int` variable, `RetVal`, for use in capturing the return value from the `puts()` function.

4 Request for Input

The program instructs the computer to tell you to enter your name. The computer displays the message `Enter your name :` onto the screen using the `printf()` function. The computer then waits for the input of your name with the `scanf()` function. After you enter your name, the computer stores your name in the `String` variable.

5 Output Message

The program tells the computer to print the message `Your name is :` to the screen using the `printf()` function. You are probably still wondering exactly how the `printf()` function works? Hold on for a few more lessons—we get to that function in Lesson 59.

6 Outputting a String

The program now instructs the computer to output the variable `String` to the screen using the `puts()` function with the string to print as the parameter. The computer accesses the block of memory marked for `String` and reads it one character at a time. As the computer reads the variable's block of memory, it writes each character to the screen starting at the last location of the cursor.

While reading the variable `String`, the computer looks for the null terminator. When the computer reaches the null terminator for `String`, the null terminator is replaced with a carriage return-line feed—the equivalent of pressing the Enter key on your keyboard.

7 Return Value

If the function `puts()` is successful in writing the variable `String` to the screen, it returns a non-negative value to the `RetVal` variable. If, for some reason, the function is unsuccessful in writing to the screen, the returned value is –1.

Preprocessor   Reserved words   Identifiers and symbols   Strings and numbers   Comments

Outputting Characters

```
1   #include <stdio.h>

2   main()
    {
        /*Declare two variables*/
3       char     CharVar;
        int      RetVal;

4       /*Request user input for the CharVar*/
        printf("Enter your choice (Y/N) : ");
        scanf("%c",&CharVar);

5       /*Print a format string to the screen along
            with the entered selection*/
        printf("Your choice is  :  ");
        RetVal = putchar(CharVar);

6       /*Print the value returned by putchar() to
            the screen*/
7       printf("\nReturned Value is '%d'\n", RetVal);
    }
```

Outputting characters is just as simple as outputting strings. The one thing to keep in mind is that a character is a single char data type while a string is a contiguous array of chars terminated by the null, \0, character. The reason for using putchar() over puts() is based on whether you want to use a two-char string to output one character—one char for the character and one for the null terminator—or simply use a single char. Ease of use and memory usage are important considerations.

1 Include Statement

The #include statement tells the compiler that the named files should be included into the code.

2 Program Entry Point

The main() statement is the program's entry point and tells the C compiler where execution begins.

3 Declarations

To use the `putchar()` function you must declare at least one `char` variable. In this lesson, the program declares a variable named `CharVar` of type `char`. The program also declares an `int` variable, `RetVal`, for use in capturing the return value from the `putchar()` function.

4 Request for Input

The program instructs the computer to tell you to make a choice. The computer displays the message `Enter your choice (Y/N) :` on the screen using the `printf()` function. The computer then waits for the input of your choice with the `scanf()` function. After you enter the character, the computer stores your choice in the `CharVar` variable.

5 Output Message

The program tells the computer to print the message `Your choice is :` to the screen using the `printf()` function.

6 Outputting a Character

The program now instructs the computer to output the variable `CharVar` to the screen using the `putchar()` function with the character to print as the parameter. The computer accesses the block of memory marked for `CharVar`, reads it, then writes it to the screen starting at the last location of the cursor. Because the character is singular, the computer does not search for a null terminator or any other termination value. The computer uses that single character and prints that to the screen.

If you should, for some reason, want to use `putchar()` to output a single character of a string, you can do that easily. Recall that a string is an array of characters and you can access one element of the array by providing an index. So, you can access one element of a string and print it using `putchar()` by `putchar(String[3]);`. The represented statement prints the fourth character of the string variable `String`.

7 Return Value

If the function `putchar()` is successful in writing the variable `CharVar` to the screen, it returns the numeric equivalent of the character entered to the `RetVal` variable. If, for some reason, the function is unsuccessful in writing to the screen, the returned value is –1.

LESSON 59

Formatted Output

```
#include <stdio.h>

main()
{
    /*Declare three variables*/
    char      String[20] = "chickens";
    int       IntVar = 10;
    float     FloatVar = 25.38;

    /*Print the formatted string to the screen*/

    printf("Them there %s cost $%4.2f for %d of
them.\n",String, FloatVar, IntVar);
}
```

1

2

3

You have seen, thus far, how to output simple strings and characters without any particular format. With the functions you have seen for screen output, you have to call each of the functions once for every string or character you wish to output. This lesson shows you how to format information going to the screen and how to output multiple variables in one function call. This type of output is quite useful in user interface development.

WHAT DOES IT MEAN?

A *user interface* is any device, such as a screen, keyboard, printer, or mouse, that enables the user to control information input and output with a computer.

1 Program Entry Point

The `main()` statement is the program's entry point and tells the C compiler where execution begins.

2 Declarations

This program declares and initializes three variables. The first variable, `String`, is a string 20 `char` long, initialized to the word *chicken*. The second variable, `IntVar`, is an `int` and is initialized to the value 10. The third, and final variable, `FloatVar`, is a `float` and is initialized to the value 25.38. When you initialize a variable in the declaration section of a program, the computer first allocates the variable, then places this value into the block of memory for the variable.

3 Formatted Output

The `printf()` function enables you to print formatted variables to the screen. Formatting statements enable you to take a number and set the maximum number of decimal places for the number as well as justification and leading zeros. You also can take a string and justify it, print integer values, and provide text on the screen as part of the output. In your program, the statement `printf("Them there %s cost $%4.2f for %d of them.\n", String, FloatVar, IntVar);` prints the message `Them there chickens cost $25.38 for 10 of them`. So, how do you get that message from that function?

You can see the text in the function that shows up in the message such as `Them there...`. This text is taken as literals and is printed to the screen the same way you place it into the format string. Such text is placed into a `printf()` function to provide meaningful output to a user.

The `%s` is a format specifier that tells the computer that a null-terminated string is placed at this point. All format specifiers are preceded by a percent sign and also can represent `float`, `%f`, `int`, `%d`, and `char`, `%c`. The format specifiers are placeholders for the variables located at the end of the function. For this program, the `%s` relates to the `String` variable, `%f`, relates to the `FloatVar` variable, and `%d` relates to the `IntVar`.

For the `%f` specifier, notice that `4.2` is entered in the middle of the specifier. This information tells the computer that it is to limit the output of the `float` to four whole values before the decimal and two decimal values after. You also have the capability to justify and pad the output with zeros, spaces, or any other character you want.

Notice the `\n` escape sequence at the end of the format string. This represents a carriage return-line feed, just like hitting Enter. After this string is printed, it brings the cursor down to the next line.

The variables are stored in what is called a *variable argument list*. The argument list, noted by `...` in programming reference manuals outlining the C function definitions, enables you to enter an undefined number of variables. For every format specifier in the `printf()` output string, you must have one variable in the variable argument list. Each entry in the list must also be in the order of the format specifiers in the output string.

WHAT DOES IT MEAN?

A *variable argument list* helps you to enter an undefined number of elements for a given function. The term *variable* in this sense is not a block of memory, but instead refers to the fact that the list of arguments is variable in length.

LESSON 60

Outputting to a String

```
#include <stdio.h>
main()
{
    /*Declare an output string and three other
       variables*/
    char    OutString[50];
    char    String[20] = "chickens";
    int     IntVar = 10;
    float   FloatVar = 25.38;

    /*Write the formatted string to the output
       string*/
    sprintf(OutString,"Them there %s cost
$%4.2f for %d of them.\n",
       String, FloatVar, IntVar);

    /*Print the string to the screen*/
    puts(OutString);

}
```

Not only can you output formatted strings to the screen, but you also can write a formatted string into another string. Why would you want to write a string into a string? Sounds a little redundant, but sometimes there is a need to write formatted information to a string. Uses for preformatted strings include output to printers, user interface aesthetics, message passing between machines on a network, and message passing between applications. Most of these uses are beyond the scope of this book, but printer output is covered later.

1 Include Statement

The #include statement tells the compiler that the named files should be included into the code.

2 Program Entry Point

The main() statement is the program's entry point and tells the C compiler where execution begins.

3 Declarations

This program declares and initializes four variables. The first variable is a string, OutString, allocated for 50 chars. The second variable, `String`, is a string, 20 `char`s long, initialized to the word `chickens`. The third variable, `IntVar`, is an `int` and is initialized to the value `10`. The final variable, `FloatVar`, is a `float` and is initialized to the value `25.38`.

4 Formatted Strings

The `sprintf()` statement enables you to print variables to a string in the same manner as `printf()` prints to the screen. The entire formatted string is written to the variable `OutString` rather than to the screen. Notice that the entire function call is identical to the `printf()` statement except for the first parameter. This parameter is now the string variable `OutString` that you declared earlier.

All formatting characters and rules apply to `sprintf()` as they do to `printf()`. You can print all of the different data types, escape sequence, and literal strings to an output string. All of this information can then, as part of the output string, be sent to its destination as a whole, formatted for the receiving device or application.

5 Output

Now that you have a formatted string, you can use the simple `puts()` function to write the string to the screen. Notice that the call to the `puts()` is no different than the call used in an earlier lesson—the main difference is the string to be output. The string, `OutString`, is already formatted and the `puts()` function is merely placing it on the screen like a normal string.

If you have to, you can use the `printf()` function to print `OutString` as part of another format string. Why? Occasionally, you might have two or three formatted strings, such as `OutString`. You can take all these strings and combine them into one preformatted output string. This type of situation helps you to take, for example, a `float` and add a dollar sign and justification, then print that newly formatted currency string to the screen as part of another message.

> **Another way to convert data types!**
>
> An interesting use for the `sprintf()` function is type conversion. You have the ability to print `floats`, `ints`, and `doubles` to a string using format specifiers. This helps you to easily convert any of the numeric data types into a string without specifically using the type conversion functions provided with the C programming language.

WHY WORRY?

It is not unusual for the output string to be overwritten beyond its boundaries because the length of the formatted string varies by the information placed into the format specifiers. Make sure that the length of the output string is at least large enough to hold the formatted string to be output.

LESSON 61

Getting a String

```c
#include <stdio.h>
main()
{
    /*Declare one variable*/
    char        String[30];

    /*Request user input for the String*/
    printf("Enter your name : ");
    gets(String);

    /*Print a format string requesting input.
      Retrieve input from the user*/
    printf("\nYour name is  :  ");
    puts(String);
}
```

1
2
3
4
5

You can put information on the screen, but where does that information come from? The input portion of a program is provided by you or some other mechanism. What you have to do is provide some mechanism inside of a program that accepts input. In C, there are almost as many input routines as there are output routines for every type of data type in the language. Take it a little at a time and look at one of the basic ones used here that help you to enter a string from the keyboard. The `gets()` function is one of the functions that enables keyboard input of strings from a user.

1 Include Statement

The `#include` statement tells the compiler that the named files should be included into the code.

2 Program Entry Point

The `main()` statement is the program's entry point and tells the C compiler where execution begins.

3 Declarations

The program tells the computer to allocate memory for a string variable called `String` consisting of 30 `char`s. This variable is used to accept input from the keyboard through the `gets()` function.

4 Getting a String

The gets() function works just like the puts() function except in reverse. You provide a variable into which the function can place a string, such as String. The function, when called, waits until you enter data and/or press the Enter. The reason for the indecision is that if you press Enter without entering text, the function simply stores nothing in the string variable String.

When you enter a string, the function stores the string into String. Pressing Enter ends the control of that function and enables the computer to continue through the remainder of the code. The function takes the carriage return-line feed that was placed in the string when you pressed Enter and replaces it with a null character.

5 Output

Now that you have a string, you can use the simple puts() function to write the string to the screen. This function, the reverse of gets(), takes the string information stored at the block of memory marked for String and places it on the screen. The null terminator, originally placed into the string by gets(), is replaced by a carriage return-line feed.

WHY WORRY?

Make sure that the input string used with gets() is at least as long as the maximum size string you want to enter—plus one. If you write over the end of the string you could be writing over other variables, operating system information, or code portions of your program.

Getting a Character

```c
#include <stdio.h>
main()
{
    /*Declare one variable*/
    char        CharVar;

    /*Request user input for the CharVar*/
    printf("Enter your choice (Y/N) : ");
    CharVar=(char)getchar();

    /*Print a string to the screen along with
        the entered selection*/
    printf("Your choice is  :  %c", CharVar);
}
```

1 **2** **3** **4** **5**

Once again, retrieving a single character from the keyboard provides a method of input for the user. As you have seen in previous lessons, there are numerous ways of reading a character from the screen. There is, however, a simple function that handles that operation as well. The getchar() function reads a character from the keyboard and places it into a variable that you provide. Such an input method is provided to enable you to have menu-driven systems and user-selectable options such as Y, N, X, and so on.

1 Include Statement

The #include statement tells the compiler that the named files should be included into the code.

2 Program Entry Point

The main() statement is the program's entry point and tells the C compiler where execution begins.

3 Declarations

The program tells the computer to allocate memory for one char variable called CharVar. This variable is used to accept input from the keyboard through the getchar() function.

4 Getting a Character

The program tells the computer to print the message `Enter your choice (Y/N) :` to the screen using the `printf()` function. The computer then waits for you to enter a character with the `getchar()` function.

Notice how `getchar()` is called as compared to any other function you have seen thus far. Rather than passing a parameter to the function, you set a variable equal to the function. In this case, `CharVar = (char) getchar();`. When you enter a character at the keyboard and press Enter, the function reads that character from the keyboard and returns that character to `CharVar`.

This program is the perfect place to use typecasting. When the `getchar()` function returns a value, this value is type `int`. Recall that the `int` is a two-byte data type while the `char`, `CharVar`, is only a single byte. By typecasting the returned `int` value of the `getchar()` function into a `char`, you can set the value of `CharVar` equal to the value of `getchar()`. So, why typecast rather than simply use an `int` variable? You might have to use the `char` data type elsewhere and would have to typecast anyway.

5 Output

The program tells the computer to output the message `Your choice is :`, followed by your choice, to the screen using the `printf()` function. Now that you have seen how the `printf()` function works, it is easy to see that the format string is telling the computer to print a `char` data type with the `%c` format specifier.

Another way that you could have printed the character `CharVar` is using the `putchar()` function with which you are familiar. This function would have simply placed the character on the screen at the last location of the cursor.

LESSON 63

Formatted Input

```
1    #include <stdio.h>

2    main()
     {
         /*Declare four variables*/
         char      String[20];
3        int       IntVar;
         float     FloatVar;
         char      CharVar;

4        /*Read a formatted string from the keyboard*/
         scanf("%c %s %d %f" ,&CharVar,String,&IntVar,
             &FloatVar);

5        /*Print the format string to the screen*/
         printf("CharVar:'%c' String: '%s' IntVar:'%d'
             FloatVar:'%f'\n",
                 CharVar,String,IntVar,FloatVar);
     }
```

For now, you can read strings and chars from the keyboard and store them into variables. But, how do you read ints, floats, doubles, or any other data type? With the simple gets() and getchar(), you can read one value at a time; but, how can you read multiple values and store them into variables? Quite simple actually—use the scanf() function. The scanf() function provides you with formatted input, much like printf()'s formatted output, to read and store many different data types in many different formats.

1 Include Statement

The #include statement tells the compiler that the named files should be included into the code.

2 Program Entry Point

The main() statement is the program's entry point and tells the C compiler where execution begins.

3 Declarations

The program tells the computer to allocate four variables. The first is a simple string called

`String` consisting of 20 `char`s. The second is `IntVar` of the `int` data type. The third is called `FloatVar` of the `float` data type. The final variable declared is `CharVar` of the `char` data type.

4 Formatted Input

The `scanf()` function helps you to format the input from the keyboard. This particular usage tells the computer to accept a `char( %c )`, a `string(%s,)` an `int( %d )`, and a `float( %f )`. The variables into which the given data types are placed are listed in the variable argument list of the function. The variables are listed in the order of their type in relation to the format string.

When you enter values into the given format string, you first enter a character followed by a space. You then enter a string followed by a space, then an integer, and then a floating point decimal. After you have entered that final value and press Enter, the values are placed into the variables.

One thing to remember when entering strings using `scanf()` is that you can only enter one word per `%s` format specifier. If you enter a string containing spaces, the `scanf()` function uses all of the characters up to the space character. For this example code, if you enter two words for the `%s`, the first word is placed into `String` and the second ends up being placed into `IntVar`. If you want to capture the two words, you must provide two variables for storage of both words so that the function can break the string at the spaces and place the two words into the variables.

WHY WORRY?

If you should happen to skip an entry, or inadvertently enter a wrong value into the formatted input stream, the function will still try to convert the value you enter and exit until you enter all of the values.

5 Formatted Output

Here is that `printf()` function again! The program uses the variables that you just read in with the `scanf()` function. The values are read from each variable and, based on the format specifier, the information is printed to the screen. The format string precedes each value's output with identifying literal text to mark the variables' output.

LESSON 64

Reading from a String

```c
#include <stdio.h>

main()
{
    /*Declare five variables*/
    char    String[50];
    char    FName[10];
    char    MName[10];
    char    LName[10];
    int     Age;

    /*Get the name and age of the user from the
      keyboard*/
    printf("Please enter your full name followed by
        your age : ");
    gets(String);

    /*Read the string and parse it into variables*/
    sscanf(String,"%s %s %s %d",FName,MName,LName,
        &Age);

    /*Print the variables to the screen*/
    printf("First:'%s' Middle: '%s' Last:'%s' Age:
        '%d'\n",
            FName,MName,LName,Age);
}
```

1

2

3

4

A final but important method of input is through the use of strings using sscanf(). You can pass a string to a program and have it sift out all of the values and place them into variables. This can be used for, as discussed with sprintf(), networks and application to application information transfer. One of the more user specific applications where sscanf() can be used is with the entry of your name. Enter your entire name and let the program break out your first, middle, and last names for storage in, for example, a database.

1 Declarations

The program tells the computer to allocate memory for five variables. The `String` variable is declared as being a 50 `char` string. The `Fname`, `MName`, `LName` variables are all declared as 10 `char` strings and are for the storage of the extracted name information from the `String` variable. The final variable, `Age`, is an `int` and is used to store the age that you enter from the keyboard into `String`.

2 Input

The program first tells the computer to prompt you for your name and age with the message `Please enter your full name followed by your age :`. The program then calls `gets()` to get a string from the keyboard. After you enter your full name—first, middle, and last—and age, separated by spaces, then press Enter, the computer stores the information you entered into `String`.

3 Reading from a String

Notice that the call to `sscanf()` is identical to `scanf()`, except that the first parameter is the input string for the function. In `scanf()`, the input came from the keyboard while `sscanf()` gets its information from `String`.

The format specifiers in the format string read in the information and store it into the variables in the variable argument list. The first three specifiers, `%s`, read strings out of `String` and place the information into the three string variables by position. The final specifier, `%d`, reads the age from `String` and places the information into the `Age` variable.

4 Output

The information extracted from `String` and placed into `FName`, `MName`, `LName`, and `Age` is printed to the screen using the `printf()` function. There are literal text labels printed before each variable's output to mark the variable's information.

> **NOTE**
>
> As with the `sprintf()` function, you can perform type conversion with `sscanf()`. You can read `floats`, `ints`, and `doubles` from a string and, by using the format specifiers, convert the string into the specified data type. The conversion then places the new value into its respective variable in the variable argument list.

PART 11

File Input/Output

Let's say you have a large amount of information stored in the computer's memory and you need to shut down the machine for the day—time to go home. If you shut down the machine, then surely everything in memory is lost! When you return in the morning you have to reenter all of that information again and begin where you left off. Quite a bit of time wasted! So, why don't you take a look at possibly saving this information somehow. Save it on a disk perhaps? You also could print the information to have some sort of hard copy backup. This way you can save the data to a disk, load it back in, and keep printouts of everything—very useful. So how can you do all this?

File input/output is the process of saving information to a disk in the form of files and reading information back into memory from the files. All file input and output is handled in a manner similar to that of screen input and output. The computer reads the information to be output from variables that you supply. It then interacts with the computer through the C run-time libraries and outputs the information to the disk in the specified file. Reading information from a file is accomplished by providing the computer with variables in which to place the information it reads from a disk-based file.

Information input and output with a file is an integral part of many programs that you purchase today. Even if you do not directly save information to a file, such as a letter or a database, the program is working with files for configuration information and memory management operations.

Most programs have configuration files they use when they start up. When you exit a program, it usually saves its current state to the configuration file. When the program is run again, the configuration file is read and the program conforms to the information it reads from the files.

If the program is designed as such, when it is started and running it uses the disk to save blocks of memory. This type of operation is called *paging* and provides a means of running a program that is otherwise larger than your machine can load into memory. The program loads chunks of a file into memory when they are needed and can save blocks of memory out to disk when they are no longer in use. The points to pay attention to here are the ideas of loading and saving blocks of memory on the disk using standard C function calls. The program doesn't care what data types are located within the block of memory it

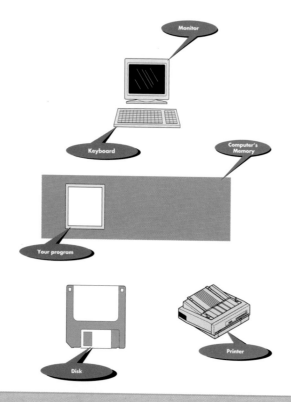

saves or loads; it deals with memory as contiguous bytes.

The other use for file input and output is when you save, for example, a spreadsheet or a word processing document to disk. You tell the program the name of the file in which to save the document and the program saves the information to that file on the disk. Printing is similar to saving a file to disk in that you tell the program, essentially, to save the information to the printer. The program then reads the information for the document or spreadsheet from memory and writes it to the printer.

The C language enables you to look at a printer as though it were a file. You can simply dump information to the printer, as you would to a file, and this information is printed. You can do the same for many other devices such as plotters and communications devices such as modems.

There are numerous functions available for the input and output of information with files and printers. You can input, as well as output, formatted and unformatted information. For files, you have access to the `fprintf()`, `fscanf()`, `fread()`, and `fwrite()` functions.

You have already seen forms of the `fprintf()` and `fscanf()` functions in previous lessons. Both of these functions enable you to perform formatted input and output with files and printers. For the printer, this is very important to properly format, for example, reports and other documents.

For standard files, you can use formatted input and output to make the files readable, but the `fread()` and `fwrite()` functions give you the option to also output unformatted data in a method where the program is not concerned about the data type. `fwrite()` takes blocks of memory and writes them to disk in a generic byte-by-byte fashion. The `fread()` function reads in chunks of a file, byte-by-byte again, and loads them into memory.

Many programs use `fread()` and `fwrite()` for file input and output because it is faster and conserves much more space than using formatted output to a file. Also, because the information saved to a file using `fwrite()` is merely a mirror image of the memory it was saved from, it is easier to save large heterogeneous structures from your programs. Recall that a heterogeneous structure is composed of many different data types. If you have to save each individual member of a heterogeneous structure to a file, this could take a lot of code to format and write the data using `fprintf()`, for example. With `fwrite()`, you simply take the block of memory reserved for the structure and write every byte from that block to disk.

Most of the material in this part has been introduced in other parts of this book. The primary difference in the information that is presented in this part is that input and output is redirected from the keyboard and screen to files that reside on your hard drive and to devices like your printer.

Opening and Closing Files

```
1  ──►#include <stdio.h>

2  ──►main()
     {
         /*Declare two variables*/
3        FILE      *outfile;
         char      FName[20] = "TESTFILE.DAT";

4        /*Open a file for reading and writing.
     Create if nonexistent*/
         outfile = fopen(FName,"w+");

5        /*Close the file*/

         fclose(outfile);
     }
```

Before you can ever read or write information between a program and a disk, you have to open a file. Just like a door—you have to know which door to go through, open the door, go through it, then close it. With a file, you locate it, open it, use it, then close it again. Opening a file is very simple with the `fopen()` function, while closing is performed by the `fclose()` function. The C run-time library handles all operations between your computer and your program's code. All you have to do is tell the computer what to read and write—and off you go.

1 Include Statement

The `#include` statement tells the compiler that the named files should be included into the code.

2 Program Entry Point

The `main()` statement is the program's entry point and tells the C compiler where execution begins.

3 Declarations

The program declares two variables—one of the data types is new to you at this point. The first variable is called `outfile` and is a pointer to a `FILE` data type. The `FILE` data type is a structure containing information about the file, including the current location with the file and the filename. The second variable, FName, is a 20-char string and is initialized to the name of the file to be opened by the program.

4 Opening a File

The fopen() function is called to open a file. The first parameter passed is the FName variable containing the name of the file to be opened. You can call the file anything you want as long as it follows the standards of filenames on a PC. If the filename is invalid, you will not be able to open the specified file. If the file is opened, a pointer to the file's information structure is returned to outfile. If the file, for some reason, cannot be opened, the value of outfile is set to zero.

The second parameter is the file access type. The type provided as part of this program is w+ which tells the computer to open a file with the name in FName for read/write access. If the file already exists, its contents are destroyed, otherwise a new file is created. A second access type is r+ which opens a file for read/write access only if the file already exists. A third type is a+ for append access—writing at the end of the file. If the file already exists then that file is used, otherwise a new file is created for appending.

> **NOTE**
>
> Filenames on a PC must follow an 8.3 approach. The 8 means that the main part of the filename can only be eight characters maximum while the 3 means that you can only have three characters for your extension—the characters after the period. Filenames may not contain spaces, commas, backslashes, or periods—except for the one preceeding the extension. A filename also may not be any of the computer's reserved names such as CLOCK$, AUX, COMx, LPTx, NUL, or PRN.

5 Closing a File

The program calls the function fclose() to close the file noted in the file variable outfile. The function tells the computer to perform an update of the file information including the file size and end-of-file marker. When you run the program, look for the file TESTFILE.DAT on your system to verify that the file was created.

WHY WORRY?

Always close a file that you have opened!!! The computer has to update the information on the disk and mark the end of the file. If you do not close files that you have opened, the information in the file will be lost.

LESSON 66

Formatted Output to a File

```
1   #include <stdio.h>

2   main()
    {
        /*Declare five variables*/
        char     String[20] = "chickens";
3       int      IntVar = 10;
        float    FloatVar = 25.38;
        FILE     *outfile;
        char     FName[20] = "TESTFILE.DAT";

4       /*Open a file for reading and writing. Create if
           nonexistent*/
        outfile = fopen(FName,"w+");

5       /*Print the format string to the file*/
        fprintf(outfile,"Them there %s cost $%4.2f for %d
           of them.\n",
               String, FloatVar, IntVar);

6       /*Close the file*/
        fclose(outfile);
    }
```

You have already been exposed to formatted output with the printf() and sprintf() statements. Take a look now at the same type of formatting, but directed to a file. This type of output is useful in reports, databases, and printing.

1 Include Statement

The #include statement tells the compiler that the named files should be included into the code.

2 Program Entry Point

The main() statement is the program's entry point and tells the C compiler where execution begins.

3 Declarations

You have already seen this example with `printf()`, so you know how the variables `String`, `IntVar`, and `FloatVar` are used. The two variables that are new here are `outfile` and `FName`. The `outfile` variable is a `FILE` data type and is used to hold the pointer for the file to be opened. This file is named in the 20-`char` string variable `Fname`.

4 Opening a File

The `fopen()` function is called to open a file. The first parameter passed is the `FName` variable containing the name of the file to be opened. The second parameter, `w+`, tells the computer to open a new file with the name in `FName` for read/write access. If the file already exists, its contents are destroyed. If the file is opened, a pointer to the file's information structure is returned to `outfile`. If the file, for some reason, cannot be opened, the value of `outfile` is set to zero.

5 Formatted Output

The `fprintf()` function enables you to print variables to the file named in `FName`. You are already familiar with formatting with the `printf()` function, and formatting is identical with this form of file output. In fact, the only difference between `printf()` and `fprintf()` is that the first parameter of `fprintf()` has a file variable in it and all formatted output goes to the file instead of the screen.

When `fprintf()` is called, it tells the computer the file in which to write the formatted information. The computer writes the formatted information to `outfile` onto the disk in an area reserved for the file when you opened it.

6 Closing a File

The program calls the function `fclose()` to close the file noted in the file variable `outfile`. The function tells the computer to perform an update of the file information including the file size and end-of-file marker.

To see the information in the file, load the file TESTFILE.DAT into a text editor. You should see `Them there chickens cost $25.38 for 10 of them.` in the file — the same output you saw in the `printf()` example of Lesson 59.

Writing Blocks to a File

```c
#include <stdio.h>

main()
{
    /*Declare three variables*/
    char      Buffer[50] = "This is a test to be
        written as a block";
    FILE      *outfile;
    char      FName[20] = "TESTFILE.DAT";

    /*Open a file for reading and writing. Create if
        nonexistent*/
    outfile = fopen(FName,"w+");

    /*Print the buffer to the file*/

    fwrite(Buffer,sizeof(Buffer),1,outfile);
    /*Close the file*

    fclose(outfile);
}
```

1

2

3

4

One of the more useful methods of file output is that of writing blocks of information to a file. As you saw with fprintf(), you can write strings to a file, but there are times where you might need to write a block of memory containing a structure, an array, or something that does not fit nicely into a standard C data type. The function fwrite() takes care of this for you by enabling you to write generic blocks of information to a specified file.

1 Declarations

The program tells the computer to allocate memory for three variables. The first variable, called Buffer, is 50 chars in length and is initialized to a value that is written to the file to be opened. The second variable, outfile, is a FILE data type and is used to hold the pointer for the file to be opened. This file to be opened is named in the 20-char string variable Fname.

2 Opening a File

The fopen() function is called to open a file. The first parameter passed is the FName variable containing the name of the file to be opened.

The second parameter, `w+`, tells the computer to open a new file with the name in `FName` for read/write access.

3 Block Write

The program calls to the `fwrite()` function to write the variable `Buffer` out to the opened file. The first parameter is the variable, `Buffer`, containing the information to be written out to the file. The second parameter contains the size of the block of memory to be written. In this case, the block of memory is marked by the variable `Buffer`. The third parameter is the number of blocks of memory of the size provided in the second parameter to be written. With this parameter you can write, for example, 10 blocks of two bytes each or, in this program, one block of 50 bytes. The final parameter is the file pointer `outfile` containing the information for the opened file.

Unlike the `fprintf()` function, `fwrite()` writes data to an opened file regardless of the type. The function sees the block of memory as a contiguous block of bytes and not as `chars`, `floats`, `ints`, or any other data type. If you are, for example, handling structures in your program for names and addresses, you can save the structures to the file without concern for the internal types that make up the structure.

4 Closing a File

The program calls the function `fclose()` to close the file noted in the file variable `outfile`. The function tells the computer to perform an update of the file information, including the file size and end-of-file marker.

To see the information in the file, load the file TESTFILE.DAT into a text editor. You should see `This is a test to be written as a block` in the file. You may also see some other characters following the string. These characters are located at the end of `Buffer` and are not necessarily part of the string. What is happening is that the `fwrite()` function is taking the entire `Buffer` from memory and writing it out. If you said, for example, in parameter two, `strlen(Buffer)`, you would only get the string up to the null character; however, `sizeof(Buffer)` returns the entire `Buffer` up to the 50th character, regardless of the null terminator.

Formatted Input from a File

```c
#include <stdio.h>

main()
{
    /*Declare four variables*/
    char      FstName[10];
    char      LstName[10];
    FILE      *infile;
    char      FName[20] = "TESTFILE.DAT";

    /*Open a file for reading only. */
    infile = fopen(FName,"r");

    /*Read the string from the file and parse it into
        variables*/
    fscanf(infile,"%s %s",FstName,LstName);

    /*Close the file*/
    fclose(infile);

    /*Print the variables to the screen*/
    printf("First:'%s'    Last:'%s'\n",FstName,
        LstName);
}
```

1
2
3
4
5

Formatted input from a file is very important for applications that, for example, use report files for temporary transaction files for database management applications. A transaction file is a small file created as users enter information into an entry screen. At certain intervals, or during a daily processing period, the transaction file is read from the disk into the computer's memory. The computer then takes this information and shuffles it off to a database for permanent storage. For simplicity, the transaction file is created using fprintf() function calls to provide a specific format for storage. The fscanf() function can then read this information from the file in the format generated by the fprintf().

1 Declarations

The computer is told to allocate memory for four variables. The variables FstName and LstName are allocated for 10 chars each. These variables are to be used to store the information that you read in from the file. The infile variable is a FILE data type and contains the information for the file name in FName that you read from.

2 Opening a File

The fopen() function is called to open a file. The first parameter passed is the FName variable containing the name of the file to be opened. The second parameter, r, tells the computer to open a new file with the name in FName for read access only. In this access mode, if the file does not exist, the file is not created and a value of 0 is returned to infile.

The file TESTFILE.DAT should be created before you run the program. Simply open a text editor and enter, for example, Harry Smith on the first line of the editor window. Now save the information to the file TESTFILE.DAT.

3 Formatted Input From a File

Notice that the call to fscanf() is identical to sscanf(), except that the first parameter is the file pointer for the file to be read from rather than a string. The format specifiers in the format string read in the information and store them into the variables in the variable argument list. The specifiers, %s, read strings out of infile and place the read information into the string variables by position.

4 Closing a File

The program calls the function fclose() to close the file noted in the file variable infile. In this situation, the file pointer infile is merely deallocated and the file is freed—thus closed.

5 Output

The information extracted from infile and placed into FstName and LstName are printed to the screen using the printf() function. There are literal text labels printed before each variable's output to mark the variable's information. If you used the example name Harry Smith, you see the message First:'Harry' Last:'Smith'.

Preprocessor   Reserved words   Identifiers and symbols   Strings and numbers   Comments

Reading Blocks from a File

```c
#include <stdio.h>

main()
{
    /*Declare three variables*/
    char      Buffer[50] ;
    FILE      *infile;
    char      FName[20] = "TESTFILE.DAT";

    /*Open a file for reading.*/
    infile = fopen(FName,"r");


    /*Read the file to the buffer*/
    fread(Buffer,sizeof(Buffer),1,infile);

    /*Close the file*/
    fclose(infile);

    /*Output the buffer to the screen*/
    printf("Buffer : '%s'\n",Buffer);

}
```

1
2
3
4

Not only can you write generic blocks of data out to a file but, you can read them. The function `fread()` enables you to read a chunk of information from a file, regardless of the data types, and place the information in memory. You have the ability, with `fread()`, to read in structures and arrays in one function call just as `fwrite()` can write them out to the file.

1 Opening a File

The `fopen()` function is called to open a file. The first parameter passed is the `FName` variable containing the name of the file to be opened. The second parameter, `r`, tells the computer to open a new file with the name in `FName` for read access only. In this access mode, if the file does not exist the file is not created and a value of 0 is returned to `infile`.

The file TESTFILE.DAT should be created before you run the program. Simply open a text editor and enter, for example, `This is a test` on the first line of the editor window. Now save the information to the file TESTFILE.DAT.

2 Block Read

The program calls to the `fread()` function to read the variable `Buffer` out of the opened file. The first parameter is the variable, `Buffer`, in which the read information is placed. The second parameter contains the size of the block of memory to be read. Read in a chunk of the file not exceeding the size of the buffer—thus, `sizeof(Buffer)`. The third parameter is the number of blocks of memory of the size provided in the second parameter to be read. With this parameter you can read, for example, 25 blocks of 2 bytes each or one block of 50 bytes, as long as it all fits into `Buffer`. The `fread()` function reads in the number of bytes specified in parameters one and two or until the end of the file is reached—whichever comes first. The final parameter is the file pointer `infile` containing the information for the opened file.

Unlike the `fscanf()` function, `fread()` reads data from an opened file regardless of the type. The function sees the file as a contiguous block of bytes and not as `chars`, `floats`, `ints`, or any other data type. If you are, for example, handling heterogeneous structures in your program for names and addresses, you can read the structures out of the file without concern for the internal types that make up the structure in which the information is being placed in memory.

3 Closing a File

The program calls the function `fclose()` to close the file noted in the file variable `infile`. The function tells the computer to perform an update of the file information including the file size and end-of-file marker. The computer then prints the contents of the buffer to the screen.

4 Output

The informamtion extracted from `infile` and placed into buffer is printed to the screen using `printf()`.

LESSON 70

Moving Around Within a File

```c
#include <stdio.h>

main()
{
        /*Declare three variables*/
        char        Buffer[3];
        FILE        *infile;
        char        FName[20] = "TESTFILE.DAT";

        /*Open a file for reading.*/
        infile = fopen(FName,"r");

        /*Seek the entered offset*/
        fseek(infile,3,SEEK_SET);

        /*Tell the current offset*/
        printf("Seeking to : %d\n", ftell(infile));

        /*Read the buffer from the file*/
        fread(Buffer,sizeof(Buffer)-1,1,infile);
        Buffer[2]='\0';

        /*Close the file*/
        fclose(infile);

        /*Output the buffer to the screen*/
        printf("Buffer : '%s'\n",Buffer);
}
```

Sometimes you need to move around within the file. When using the read and write function for file input and output, the file pointer variable tells where the next read or write occurs within the file. This type of movement within the file is important for updating database records in a disk-based database file. For example, you might want to change a person's address stored in the fourth record of a database. A database management program would use `fseek()` to go to the position at the beginning of the fourth database record and change the address as specified.

1 Opening a File

The `fopen()` function is called to open a file. The first parameter passed is the `FName` variable containing the name of the file to be opened. The second parameter, `r`, tells the computer to open a new file with the name in `FName` for read access only. In this access mode, if the file does not exist, the file is not created and a value of 0 is returned to `infile`.

2 Seeking in the File

The function call `fseek(infile,3,SEEK_SET)` tells the computer to go to the fourth byte, with respect to the beginning of `infile`. The first parameter is the file used for the seek operation. The value `3` is the offset within the file, starting at 0, to go to based on the third parameter `SEEK_SET`. The parameter `SEEK_SET`, defined in `stdio.h`, tells the computer to seek from the beginning of the file. `SEEK_END` seeks from the end of the file, and `SEEK_CUR` seeks from the current location of the file pointer within the file. The program then tells you, using `ftell()` through `printf()`, exactly where the file pointer is located at the end of the seek operation.

3 Block Read

The program calls to the `fread()` function to read the variable `Buffer` out of the opened file. The function reads only two of the three bytes of `Buffer` given by `sizeof(Buffer)-1`. The reason that you only read two bytes is that you need to reserve the third byte for a null terminator—remember strings? After the two characters are read into the buffer, the program places a null terminator at the end of the string in `Buffer`.

4 Closing a File

The program calls the function `fclose()` to close the file noted in the file variable `infile`. The function tells the computer to perform an update of the file information including the file size and end-of-file marker.

5 Output

The computer then prints the contents of the buffer to the screen.

LESSON 71

Opening a Printer Device

```c
#include <stdio.h>

main()
{
  /*Declare two variables*/
  FILE      *prtfile;
  char      FName[20] = "LPT1";

  /*Open the printer for writing*/
  prtfile = fopen(FName,"w");

  /*Close the printer*/
  fclose(prtfile);
}
```

A *peripheral* is any device that is used by a computer outside of its standard memory and microprocessor. For example, a monitor is a peripheral device, as well as a keyboard, a printer, an external disk drive, and so on.

One important output peripheral is a printer. Without a printer you could not generate reports for your boss, financial statements for your lender, or letters to your friends. You would have to either have your friends over to read the letter from the screen or send them a disk on which the letter is stored. Lessons 71 and 72 review the concepts presented in previous lessons—with a little twist.

1 Include Statement

The #include statement tells the compiler that the named files should be included into the code.

2 Program Entry Point

The main() statement is the program's entry point and tells the C compiler where execution begins.

3 Declarations

The program declares two variables for accessing the printer. The first data type is called prtfile and is a pointer to a FILE data type. The prtfile variable is used to hold information about the printer rather than a disk-based file. The second variable, FName, is a 20-char string and is initialized to LPT1 to print from printer port number 1. If your printer is connected to a different port, such as LPT2 or COM1, simply change the initialization value for FName.

4 Opening the Printer

The fopen() function is called to open the printer the same way you open a file. The first parameter passed is the FName variable containing the name of the printer port to access and open. If the printer is opened, a pointer to the printer's information structure is returned to prtfile. If the printer, for some reason, cannot be opened, the value of prtfile is set to zero.

The second parameter is w, the file access type. This parameter tells the computer to open the printer for writing only and, if it does not exist, return an error without trying to create a printer. If, however, you should open the file with w+ access and a new printer does appear—patent the process!

5 Closing a File

The program calls the function fclose() to close the printer noted in the variable prtfile. The function tells the computer to flush the buffer and close the printer port.

WHY WORRY?

Remember—always close a file that you have opened!!! This includes the printer! The computer has to flush the information to the printer and close out the port before another program can access it successfully.

WHAT DOES IT MEAN?

The references to LPT1, LPT2, and COM1 are all references to the ports, or the connections, of your computer. LPT1 and LPT2 are parallel ports used to connect to your printer. COM1 is a serial port that is used to connect to a modem or a mouse. Each of these ports is recognized by the computer. When you open a file pointer to any of these ports, the computer allows you to write to these ports just like the disk-based files in the previous lessons.

WHAT DOES IT MEAN?

When you *flush a buffer* you are forcing any information stored between the printer and your program out to the printer. This makes sure that everything sent from your program is received by the printer for printing.

Outputting to a Printer

```
1   #include <stdio.h>

2   main()
    {
        /*Declare five variables*/
        char        String[20] = "chickens";
3       int         IntVar = 10;
        float       FloatVar = 25.38;
        FILE        *prtfile;
        char        FName[20] = "LPT1";

4       /*Open the printer for writing.*/
        prtfile = fopen(FName,"w");

5       /*Print the format string to the printer*/
        fprintf(prtfile,"Them there %s cost $%4.2f for %d of
            them.\n",  String, FloatVar, IntVar);

6       /*Close the printer*/
        fclose(prtfile);
    }
```

Opening and closing a printer device doesn't do much good unless you do something with it. You can write to a printer the same way that you write to a file and to the screen. Simply call one of the file output functions and your text is printed. You have already seen this example program in previous lessons, but the difference here is in the destination of the output string.

1 Include Statement

The #include statement tells the compiler that the named files should be included into the code.

2 Program Entry Point

The main() statement is the program's entry point and tells the C compiler where execution begins.

3 Declarations

Once again, you have the variables `String`, `IntVar`, and `FloatVar` used in previous lessons. The two other variables are `prtfile` and `FName`. The `prtfile` variable is a `FILE` data type and is used to hold the pointer for the printer to be opened. This file to be opened is named in the 20-`char` string variable `FName`.

4 Opening the Printer

The `fopen()` function is called to open the printer the same way you open a file. The first parameter passed is the `FName` variable containing the name of the printer port to access and open. If the printer is opened, a pointer to the printer's information structure is returned to `prtfile`. If the printer, for some reason, cannot be opened, the value of `prtfile` is set to zero.

The second parameter is `w`, the file access type. This tells the computer to open the printer for writing only and, if it does not exist, return an error.

5 Formatted Output

The `fprintf()` function is called to send a string to the printer. When `fprintf()` is called, it tells the computer to write the formatted information to the printer. The computer then takes the formatted information and writes it to `prtfile`. The output to `prtfile` is directed to the printer causing the printer to print the string `Them there chickens cost $25.38 for 10 of them`.

6 Closing a File

The program calls the function `fclose()` to close the file noted in the file variable `prtfile`. The function tells the computer to flush the buffer and close the printer port.

If you do not close the file at the end of a print to the printer, the text may not appear on the paper. The reason is that the computer and the printer both have buffers that store information during the transfer from your program to the final paper. If you do not close the file, the last line of a printout is usually not printed. When you close the file, the computer forces all remaining information to the destination, causing the information to be printed and all buffers cleared.

> **WHAT DOES IT MEAN?**
>
> A *buffer* is a region of memory allocated for the temporary storage of information between your computer and the data's destination. The destination can be either a file or any peripheral device. The computer buffers all information to allow the device to complete operations and to keep devices from backing up when waiting for destination devices to become ready for more data.

Index

Symbols

Index